Sustainable development is a notion that must apply as much to the industrial countries of the North as to the South. This timely book argues that to convert the technologically possible into the economically feasible requires an efficiency revolution in our use of natural resources, including energy in particular. After surveying the economic instruments available — tradeable permits, pollution charges, refund systems and 'green' taxes — the authors argue that, for the business community, revenue-neutral ecological tax reform could be a much more attractive as well as effective option. It would reward long-term investment in resource-efficient technologies, including moves away from reliance on fossil fuels for our transport and energy systems. And it would provide strong enough incentives to encourage the large-scale change in private sector behaviour needed to reduce global warming and the use of non-renewable resources.

This book presents new evidence of the significant degree of fuel price elasticity that is possible in the transport sector as one example of the practical viability of these proposals. It explores the issues involved in moving the tax base away from corporation and income taxes to ecological taxes based on resource utilisation. It suggests that ecological taxes can provide a realistic policy option if introduced gradually, and in ways that are revenue-neutral, easy to administer, internationally harmonised, and combined with measures to compensate for any negative social distribution effects.

# The Authors

Professor ERNST U. VON WEIZSÄCKER held the chair of Interdisciplinary Biology at Essen University before he was appointed President of the new University of Kassel in 1975. After completing his five-year term, he served as a Director at the United Nations Center for Science and Technology for Development. In 1984 he became Director of the Institute for European Environmental Policy in Bonn. Since early 1991 he has been President of the Wuppertal Institute for Climate, Energy and the Environment.

He is a member of the Club of Rome. In 1989 he was recipient — together with the Norwegian Prime Minister, Mrs Gro Harlem Brundtland — of the Italian De Natura Prize.

He has published numerous articles, essays and books in the field of environmental policy, the theory of open systems, and technology policy. His most recent book, Earth Politics (English edition in preparation), was first published in 1989.

His co-author, JOCHEN JESINGHAUS, is an economist with the European Statistical Office, Luxembourg. He trained originally as a mechanical and process engineer before going on to study economics and political science at the University of Mannheim.

ERNST U VON WEIZSÄCKER and JOCHEN JESINGHAUS

# Ecological Tax Reform

A POLICY PROPOSAL FOR SUSTAINABLE DEVELOPMENT

ZED BOOKS

LONDON & NEW JERSEY

Institute for European Environmental Policy, Bonn
Wuppertal Institute for Climate, Energy and the Environment

A study prepared for
Dr. Stephan Schmidheiny
Chairman
The Business Council
for Sustainable Development

Ecological Tax Reform was first published by Zed Books Ltd.,
57 Caledonian Road, London N1 9BU, UK,
and 165 First Avenue, Atlantic Highlands, New Jersey 07716, USA,
in 1992

Translated by Richard Janssen

Cover designed by Andrew Corbett
Typeset and graphics by Hans Kretschmer, Wuppertal Institute
Printed and bound in the United Kingdom
by Biddles Ltd., Guildford and King's Lynn

A catalogue record for this book
is available from the British Library
US CIP is available from the Library of Congress
ISBN 1 85649 095 5 Cased
ISBN 1 85649 096 3 Limp

Ecological Tax Reform

# Table of Contents

# Preface

The majestic old sailing vessel *Stadsraad Lehmkuhl* is no doubt the gem of the Norwegian harbour of Bergen. It was during a reception given on board of this windjammer that I received Dr. Stephan Schmidheiny's agreement that he would sponsor a policy study on ecological tax reform. That was in May 1990, during the Bergen Conference, perhaps the most important regional Conference in the process of preparations for the Earth Summit, Rio de Janeiro 1992.

Stephan Schmidheiny felt, as I did, that in the global struggles towards a sustainable development the active involvement of the business community was becoming an urgent necessity. And we were both convinced that the present framework for doing business was not exactly rewarding those trying to move their companies forward on the road to sustainability. How could the framework be changed without jeopardising our prosperity? That is the big question to be put to environmental policy makers. Existing legislation which concentrates on pollution control is no satisfactory answer. It has hardly begun to influence patterns of energy and resource consumption and has created the impression that economic strength, if not material affluence, is the necessary prerequisite for environmental protection. If that was really the case, there would be no chance for environmental protection in the vast majority of countries.

It has become a necessity to come up with new policy proposals. They should create a dynamic movement in the rich countries to save natural resources used as inputs, reduce greenhouse gas emissions and waste products, and at the same time keep those countries in a healthy state. An ecological tax reform, we argue in this book, seems to be an attractive strategy in this regard. But it has met with numerous objections from different quarters. It is our hope, therefore, that a rather quick policy study could serve to clarify and resolve some of the objections.

What seems most difficult to assess is whether an ecological tax reform that is gentle enough not to cause massive disruptions, and therefore losses, in the economy is nevertheless able to steer technology and investments swiftly enough in the desired direction. Is the 'price elasticity' large enough? It has been generally believed hitherto to be very small for such important factors as fossil fuels for automobiles.

After I began working on the project at the Institute for European Environmental Policy (IEEP) in Bonn, I was singularly lucky in finding Mr. Jochen Jesinghaus, a young economist working at the University of Mannheim, who agreed to make the tax project his first priority for a number of months. He soon came up with unusual proposals to measure price elasticities in OECD countries. His comparative approach made it possible to prove (insofar as proofs are possible in the soft sciences) that the elasticity was in fact much larger than generally believed.

Our work, of which Jochen Jesinghaus took the larger share, progressed steadily and was greatly helped by the regular meetings we held in Stephan Schmidheiny's team which was coordinated by Dr. Ernst A. Brugger. I am deeply grateful to him for the excellent cooperation during almost a whole year. Also I wish to thank Irene Ring and Dr. Gerhard Maier-Rigaud of IEEP Bonn, Dr. Samuel Mauch and Rolf Iten of INFRAS, Switzerland, Dr. W. Bosshardt, Mr. O. Straub, and numerous other researchers for countless discussions. I also wish to thank Robert Molteno of Zed Books for having gone to such pains with me to transform a text which was originally addressed to German and Swiss readers into something intelligible for English-speaking and international readers. Obviously, the fine translation by Richard Janssen was a very good starting point for this work.

*Ernst U. von Weizsäcker*
Wuppertal Institute for Climate,
Energy and the Environment

# 1. Introduction: The Crisis Runs Deeper Than We Think

Sustainable development has become imperative. As the Brundtland Report [1] argues, further growth in a conventional sense will not lead to worldwide prosperity. Rather it will ultimately lead to destruction. The very basis of life and prosperity is at stake. (For further references, see note 1).

According to FAO and other sources we are losing roughly 3,000 square metres of forests *every second*. Human-made emissions of greenhouse gases have reached a rate of nearly 1,000 tons every second. Severe and unpredictable climatic changes are very likely to occur during the next century. The fertility of vast tracts of land and eventually the very inhabitability of coastal regions are endangered.

The expected change is likely to happen with such rapidity that plants which are the basis of most ecosystems will be unable to adjust or to migrate in time. Catastrophic losses of biodiversity would ensue. Already, we are probably losing some ten, possibly even 20 or more, species every day, due mostly to habitat destruction.

The ozone hole is growing. Even the London amendments to the Montreal Protocol on the protection of the ozone layer will not prevent a very serious deterioration within the coming decades. Hundreds of thousands of people, perhaps millions, are threatened by skin cancer induced by ultraviolet rays which are no longer cut out by the stratospheric ozone layer. Nobody can truly assess the long-term damage caused by ultraviolet radiation in killing substantial portions of marine plankton.

3

Non-renewable raw materials are steadily diminishing. By way of example, Fig. 1 shows — dramatised by the use of an uncommonly long time scale and, therefore, quite speculative as regards the actual quantitative figures — that the present consumption patterns for just one important commodity, petroleum, will result in hundreds of future generations having to make do entirely without it.

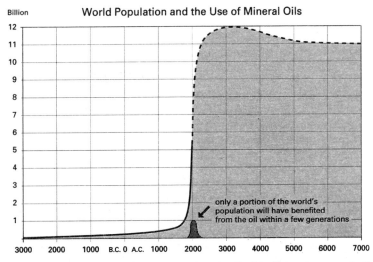

**Fig. 1:** Mankind is capable of exhausting the Earth's finite reserves of oil within just a few generations; and during this period, only a portion of the world's population will have benefited from the oil. [2]

Pollution, too, is becoming a worldwide phenomenon. Thousands of lakes and rivers are so polluted that virtually all animal life has been destroyed. Widespread air pollution is threatening human health and forests as well as other habitats. Wastes, including highly toxic wastes, are growing into unmanageable mountains. And the soils of many countries have to absorb an ever increasing load of toxic substances.

Conventional environmental policy was mostly concerned with setting standards of environmental quality or of maximum emissions per unit of a polluting source. This road has proven fundamentally unsatisfactory when considered from a global perspective. So-called 'end of the pipe' pollution control inescapably leads to add-on costs for every measure of environmental protection. This then leads to the perception by poor and rich countries that only the rich can afford stringent environmental standards. So it is almost natural that developing countries show little enthusiasm for environmental policy.

Things are getting worse. The developing countries do not see why they should be denied access to the path to prosperity taken by the industrialised countries, which also is the only path to prosperity thus far proven to exist. They envisage for themselves sharply increasing demand for resources and energy. This, by the way, is also the case in countries which have instituted effective population stabilisation programme or have otherwise achieved rapidly decreasing family sizes.

These aspirations of increasing energy demand in the developing world, not denied by any serious energy analyst in the North, are the basis of forecasts by the World Energy Conference for drastically rising world energy consumption rates — a doubling or so within some 40 years from now.

On the other hand, the Intergovernmental Panel on Climate Change (IPCC)[3] regards a major reduction, perhaps by 50 per cent, of greenhouse gas emissions as a necessity if we are to finally stabilise the global climate before a catastrophic warming may have taken place. $CO_2$, resulting mostly from the combustion of fossil fuels, is the most important greenhouse gas. An enormous gap is opening up between likely levels of $CO_2$ emissions (if no measures are taken) and the sharply reduced levels required if global warming is to be avoided. This is symbolically indicated in a qualitative manner in Fig. 2.

To try fill the gap by nuclear energy appears to be a dangerous course of action, and illusory too. It's not only nuclear safety that troubles people. Even the safest of today's reactors remain vulnerable to damage wrought in time of war and to sabotage, and hence lend themselves to being targets for blackmail. And

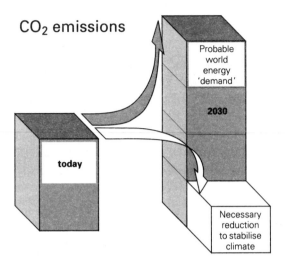

**Fig. 2:** According to World Energy Conference data, global energy consumption continues to rise unabated and will continue to stem mostly from the combustion of fossil fuels. In order to stabilise the climate at acceptable temperatures, a drastic reduction in $CO_2$ emissions would be necessary.[4]

the safe handling of very large quantities of fissionable material suitable for the manufacture of nuclear weapons that would inevitably appear on the market place is a nightmarish undertaking too. Thus the contribution of nuclear energy to the world's energy requirements will remain modest.

Fusion energy is unlikely to be available in significant quantities during the next few decades, and the hazards may well turn out to be of the same order of magnitude as with power from nuclear fission. There are the problems of enormous flows of neutrons bombarding and rendering radioactive any conceivable shielding material, and the production of huge quantities of tritium, one of the most insidiously radioactive substances.[5]

Solar energy and other sources of renewable energy have a better prospect from a technical and environmental point of view. And in certain places they have become competitive in recent years.[6] However, their general commercial viability remains limited under prevailing world market conditions. Also, they themselves will probably be seen as environmentally damaging as soon as they are produced by the gigawatt — i.e. on the huge scale that would be required.

All this means that, for many decades to come, fossil fuel will most likely continue to represent the largest part of the energy pie.

What is valid for world energy consumption is, *mutatis mutandis*, equally so for water use, raw materials consumption (on account of the impact of mining, processing, transportation, manufacture and waste products), and ecologically detrimental land use. The gap between development 'requirements' under even modest assumptions of economic growth and ecologically sustainable levels of consumption is growing ominously wide.

Conventional — end of the pipe — environmental protection measures can do very little to narrow the various gaps. In fact, we find that such classic means of controlling pollution as catalytic converters, flue gas desulfurisation, recycling and sewage treatment actually result in increased energy and materials consumption. For all its technologies and processes, conventional environmental protection looks pretty helpless in the face of the coming world challenges.

These can be expressed as follows. As long as the countries of the North persist in consuming around ten times more natural resources per capita than the developing countries, the gap will continue to grow wider and wider with the situation becoming increasing hopeless. A drastic reduction in per capita resource consumption in the North is ecologically imperative. And for the developing countries, it is the path of resource conservation — one that avoids the historical detour of the throw-away society — that will lead to the modern promised land.

Why this strong focus on resources? Have we not overcome the worry about resource depletion that was set in motion in the early 1970s by the *Limits to Growth* [7] report to the Club of Rome? Spurred on by the oil crisis, the years that followed saw a worldwide intensification of resource exploration and exploitation, conducted with the aid of hyper-modern methods. And the effort paid off. Particularly with respect to oil and gas, fears that the well would soon run dry gave way to a feeling of plenty. In fact, oil and oil shale that either had a high sulphur content or was difficult to get at was simply left in the ground because 'it just wasn't worth it'. From the early 1980s on, the limitations were primarily seen in terms of the Earth's limited capacity to absorb pollutants, while resource conservation *per se* slipped back into political obscurity.

However, the considerations set out above show that the long-term resource problem is as real as ever (see Fig. 1) and the pollution problem, due to the limited absorptive capacity of the Earth, has only become worse (see Fig. 2).

The worldwide ecological crisis is thus substantially deeper than the prevailing environmental policy debate today might lead one to believe.

Certain pioneers in the world community have recognised this. During 1984-1987, the United Nations established the World Commission on Environment and Development under the leadership of Norwegian Prime Minister Gro Harlem Brundtland. The Commission's final report, *Our Common Future*,[1] became one of the most important documents of the decade. The Brundtland Report was very well received by the United Nations General Assembly which resolved to convene the United Nations Conference for Environment and Development (UNCED).

UNCED, often called the Earth Summit, is being held in Rio de Janeiro in June 1992. It is probably the world's largest international conference ever and could prove to be one of the most important diplomatic events of human history. The challenge before the Conference is essentially the challenge outlined above. The South wants decent prospects of development and on the basis of a viable model. But there is only one development model available. Should the South, with or without aid, manage to achieve anything like present Northern consumption rates of energy and raw materials, that would inescapably jeopardise the ecological survival of the globe.

From this it follows — and this is the basic assumption of our book — that the most important contribution by the North would be to change its own model. Sustainability, then, is primarily *a task addressed to the North.*[8]

Our study, therefore, deals with the possibilities for the North of attaining a new and credible role model. The possibilities rest, so we argue, with *a revolutionary increase in resource productivity.*

To trigger off that new technological (and cultural) revolution, we propose an *ecological tax reform* which we are convinced can be tailored in such a way that it is both socially acceptable and would actually improve profitable opportunities for the business world. We think that green taxes should primarily be levied on environmentally important *input factors,* notably energy. The taxes should involve *a steady price increase of some 5 per cent annually over some 30 to 40 years* for fossil fuels and nuclear energy, as well as for other problematic natural resources. Revenue neutrality could be secured by reducing other taxes such as VAT, income taxes or corporation taxes in order to ensure that the overall tax burden on business does not increase, but is merely redistributed in such a way as to provide strong and enduring incentives to invest in new technologies geared to reducing significantly the energy and raw material inputs per given unit of output. That is the essence of our proposal.

# 2. Increasing the Productivity of Natural Resources and Energy

The imperative stated in the Introduction allows for one of two very different approaches. Either there must be a drastic reduction in per capita consumption of resources, entailing sacrifices that would extend to voluntary poverty on the part of the North. Or there must be a drastic increase in resource productivity. The first approach is obviously far less desirable than the second, and politically hopeless to boot, particularly when the second approach has yet to have even been tried.

As $CO_2$ is the most important greenhouse gas contributing to the dangers of global warming we shall first discuss what may be called $CO_2$ productivity as one illustrative example of a resource productivity that may be increased as a result of deliberate political and technological action.

$CO_2$ productivity may (and here we are disregarding the fact that GNP is a measure of turnover, not prosperity) be broadly defined as one unit of GNP per unit of $CO_2$. Assuming that global GNP were to double during the next 20 years (which would correspond to an annual growth rate of 3.5% and an increase in per capita GNP of some 1.5%, due to the fact that the population is expected to grow by about half in that time), and that global $CO_2$ emissions as a result of new policies were to be halved, then $CO_2$ productivity would have to be quadrupled during the same period.

In other words, in 20 years, each unit of $CO_2$ emission would have to result in four times more economic production than is achieved today. This corresponds to a spanking 7% annual rate of increase in $CO_2$ productivity. By way of comparison, since the oil crises of 1973-74, the GNP of the (West) German economy has grown by around 36%; in contrast to this, consumption of primary energy (which during this period went hand in hand with $CO_2$ emissions) increased by 3.7%. So, in spite of two oil crises, $CO_2$ productivity from 1973 to the present day has risen only by 31%, at an annual rate of a mere 1.6%. This rate of increase is generally viewed as being a great success, as a sign that savings in energy consumption continue to be made.

However, even with an annual increase in $CO_2$ productivity of 1.6%, $CO_2$ emissions worldwide will continue to increase rather than diminish. Merely in order to place the necessary controls on this one (albeit the most significant) greenhouse gas $CO_2$, it is obvious that the pace of our efforts to obtain sustainable development through greater efficiency will have to be considerably more ambitious than that which resulted from the dynamic of 'natural' technical progress — even under the favourable conditions of the oil price hikes of 1973 and 1979.

The conventional instruments of environmental policy are ill-suited for achieving this goal. In view of the speed and scale required, the necessary technical and social changes can hardly be achieved by setting norms. In a democracy, draconian energy saving measures would be difficult to implement, and totalitarian systems, as the post-war history of Eastern Europe in particular shows, tend to be inefficient; energy consumption per unit of production there is twice as high as in West Germany.

Trying to prescribe in detail for the next 20 years of development is to misunderstand the nature of technical and social change. Technical progress proceeds in a rather unplanned fashion. However, direction and scope are determined by signals, by no means least the signals of price, market expectations and the internal dynamic of expanding knowledge.

Market expectations depend very much on what consumers will be able to afford to pay in future, and thus once again on price signals. And progress in knowledge can also be thoroughly influenced as to its direction. Thus the expectation, widely accepted from the mid 1950s, of steadily growing energy demand played a decisive role in triggering advances in our scientific and technical knowledge concerning exploitable energy sources.

If the conviction, supported by appropriate market signals, were to prevail that $CO_2$ efficiency had to be drastically improved, we ought to be able to expect at least a certain amount of progress. The technologies are there, even today, to probably double or even triple $CO_2$ productivity — and hence create the possibility of advancing material standards of living while actually reducing this threat of global warming.

To take one example, the replacement of coal by natural gas and renewable energy sources could theoretically raise $CO_2$ productivity by 20-30%. However, that is only true if major leaking of gas can be avoided.

Increasing energy efficiency is even more important.[9] The greatest potential for improvement seems to be in the area of heating. There are already houses in existence which, aside from the natural sunlight including diffuse light, manage entirely without external heat sources. In the field of transport, fuel efficiency could easily be doubled, probably tripled. And the remaining required fuel could be at least largely extracted from renewable sources or be replaced by $CO_2$-free solar power. From the technical standpoint, a tripling of productivity is thoroughly feasible (see note 9 again).

As for electricity (and the production of electricity from coal), there is less potential for improvement. The 'simplest' way of increasing $CO_2$ productivity in this domain, the replacement of coal-fired plants with nuclear power stations is, at least politically, so controversial in most countries that it deserves at most a secondary priority. Combined heat and power (CHP), an expanded role for natural gas among the fossil fuels, combined gas and coal-fired plants could increase $CO_2$ productivity by some 30%. Another 10-30% may be achieved by reducing transmission losses as well as employing more energy-efficient machines, household appliances and light sources. Further technical progress is to be expected. Also, solar power — in the broadest sense — will play an increasingly significant role.

But achieving these potential productivity increases and successfully introducing solar energy depends to a large extent on the surrounding matrix of conditions, notably prices. Given today's low prices for oil and other fossil fuels, one can hardly expect this potential to even come close to being fully exploited. If $CO_2$ emissions, however, were to become substantially more expensive, increasing $CO_2$ productivity would become correspondingly more profitable, meaning that the increases in efficiency mapped out above would meet at least with partial success in the market place.

$CO_2$ productivity is only one example — to be sure an exceptionally important one — of the overall productivity challenge. In principle, the same things apply to energy productivity in general as apply to the special case of $CO_2$. As was stressed above, energy productivity can be substantially boosted. At the same time — depending on estimates and analysis of the ecological risks — the relative proportion of the various fuel types in use can be altered by means of regulatory targets and/or price influencing measures.

Efficiency in the use of raw materials can also be considerably enhanced by appropriately adjusting the determining parameters. It appears to be perfectly plausible that the increases in productivity necessary for sustainable prosperity can indeed be achieved, but not without bringing extensive influence to bear on the parameters within which technical and economic development takes place.

# 3. Economic Instruments of Environmental Policy

The present types of standard-setting policy and licensing procedures are inadequate in the face of the major ecological challenges confronting the planet. They have not halted the destructive trends on a global scale, and environmental policies based on such instruments invariably rank second to economic objectives in less developed countries. They should therefore be supplemented by the economic instruments of environmental policy.[10] Here, the highly efficient mechanism of the market can be applied to the environment. It can be made cheaper for participants in the market to place less of a burden on the environment and to be more economical in their use of natural resources. Wherever such market-based measures lead to increased resource efficiency, they are likely to be more acceptable than pollution control legislation both to the business community in the North and to the less developed countries.

The most important economic instruments are tradeable permits, special charges and ecological taxes.

## Tradeable Permits

If we assume that a precise ecological goal, for instance the goal of reducing $CO_2$, is scientifically justified, then logically the most sensible way of setting the framework for economic activity would be to establish permissible consumption and emission levels, and to issue permits for the total volume of such permissible consumption and emission, which could be traded on the market. The market mechanism of supply and demand would lead to a price which each consumer or emitter of pollution would have to pay in addition to the cost of the raw material procured. [11]

Ambitious $CO_2$ reduction goals would obviously make the permits rarer and dearer and would push prices up, as would any sudden peaks in demand. Conservationists would be permitted to purchase permits with no other intention than to prevent the burning of fuels, which also would lead to price increases. Speculative accumulation of permits, trade in $CO_2$ futures, even fake permits — all this is also conceivable.

To be sure, the permits model has to deal with a whole range of problems.

*First*, the scientific evidence leading to the postulated reduction goal may be weak; and those interested in less ambitious reduction goals will not hesitate to pinpoint this fact. Ultimately, the definition of the reduction goal will always be based on a *political* compromise, often a poor one. The apparent rationality of obtaining optimum results via the market can then be self-deceptive. If there is an alternative way not merely of meeting reduction goals but of actually exceeding them, then such an alternative seems preferable ecologically. And it is precisely in the hopes of finding such a way that is the driving force behind the ecological tax reform proposals in the present study.

*Second,* if, instead of weak-kneed compromises, ambitious reduction goals are agreed to, there is the danger that during periods of high demand, and particularly during economic booms, permit prices could shoot up unpredictably. The long-range calculability of input prices that is so important for investors and for swift and smooth technological development is thus lacking.

*Third,* up until now, the concept of tradeable permits has in practice been limited to *emissions,* and thus presupposes continuous, accurate and credible emission measurements. This condition can only be met in technologically highly developed societies and then only for certain pollutants. For $CO_2$ emissions one can, of course, make do with emission equivalents on the input side (carbon content of coal, oil and gas.)

In spite of these problems, price setting for $CO_2$ emissions via tradeable permits remains one of the most important policy options for limiting the greenhouse effect. Particularly on the *international* level, where the distribution of reduction obligations and/or $CO_2$ emission permits for entire countries is at issue, a model in which permits are at least initially determined by population (or the number of adults),[12] would be a highly valuable instrument for balancing North-South interests, while at the same time serving to stabilise the Earth's atmosphere at a safe level. But an international agreement that would even things out in this way is a highly remote prospect. Nor would successfully applying the permits model on the international level necessarily mean that it would be the optimum allocation instrument on the national level, where the above mentioned weaknesses are primarily relevant.

**Special Charges**

Another means of artificially raising the price of pollution, scarce resources or energy is the levying of charges, the proceeds of which are earmarked for services, remedial action or prevention in the direct context of the pollution or resource consumption concerned.

Charges can take the form of *user charges*, for example payment for public services such as waste collection or sewage. Along with their financing functions, they can also serve to influence behaviour. In such cases, they are often (e.g. Opschoor and Vos, see note 10) referred to as *effluent charges*. Examples include the Dutch, French and German waste water charges. Proceeds from them are directly applied to pollution prevention or clean-up activities.

Charges feature the twin advantages of placing a burden on the polluter and focusing financial resources directly on the environment. Thus, in terms of money expended, they exercise a double ecological influence. If one accepts that the private sector disposes of money more efficiently than the state, the influence factor can be even further enhanced if the state does not spend the money itself, but rather returns it to those in the private sector who are able to demonstrate success in ecological clean-up and prevention. In this case, one may speak of a carrot-and-stick or charge-benefit system, from which, on average, a somewhat higher degree of steering effectiveness is to be expected.

However, in terms of their total volume, earmarked charges and charge-benefit systems are subject to relatively narrow limits. In calculating the charges that are to be paid by polluters and the funds that are to be expended by the state, the burden of proof is such that it can only be met in cases where damage is thoroughly manifest and where measures for repair and prevention can be precisely justified. Furthermore, each earmarked charge means an expanded role for the public sector, an increase in bureaucracy which — to put it mildly — is unpopular today. Thus, it comes as no surprise that in none of the 14 OECD countries examined by Opschoor and Vos did revenue from earmarked charges amount to more than one tenth of one per cent of GNP. And for steering an entire economy on to a course of energy and resource efficiency, this amount is of course far too little.

Everywhere where the burden of proof can be met, environmental policy should attempt to make use of carrot-and-stick systems and earmarked charges to the extent that the economy can bear the additional costs. In situations where they can be applied they are very likely to be more efficient than conventional command and control instruments.

However, recent German experience seems to confirm that the political scope for charges that work as an additional financial burden on the private sector is very limited indeed. In 1991, for example, Minister Klaus Töpfer, who otherwise enjoyed considerable political support as a Christian Democrat from the business community, came under very severe attack following his announcement of a federal waste charge and a $CO_2$ charge.

Revenue neutrality — i.e. changes in the tax system that place no increased burden on the private sector — appears to be a very high priority for the business community. This leads to our argument for an in-depth study of an ecological tax reform.

## Ecological Tax Reform

Ecological tax reform is a different thing altogether. The idea is to put taxes on fossil fuels and nuclear energy, on water consumption, on raw materials (especially those which are likely to end up as toxic pollutants or hazardous waste), and also possibly on emissions and waste, and to reduce other taxes instead. A *revenue neutral* tax reform would observe the stipulation that the overall fiscal burden on business must not increase. Revenue neutrality has a politically important termino-logical implication: with revenue neutrality, one should not talk about environmental or 'green' taxes, but rather about *ecological tax reform*. This is likely to meet with greater political accept-ance than the term 'green' taxes, which could be understood as representing an additional burden.

Unlike earmarked charges, ecological tax reform requires *no scientific proof* of the causal chain lying between the taxed commodity or emission and the environmental damage. A government's exchequer never has to prove that any of the elements which are taxed in our society cause damage. With income taxes, VAT or corporation taxes, nobody would even dream that they are meant as a penalty against anything undesirable. Rather, human labour, the creation of added value and business activity are seen as something highly desirable for our economy. Thus, income and corporation taxes, just like the VAT in force throughout the EC, are seen by economists [13] as having a *negative* effect on the economy, albeit one which is generally accepted on account of the undisputed need for public spending.

If there is no ecological burden of proof for 'green' taxes, their acceptance in the political arena nevertheless depends

- on their ecological *plausibility,* i.e. their expected capacity to steer society in the intended direction;
- on social equity; and
- on their effects, positive or negative, on the economy.

If environmental taxes are employed by the state in such a way that other taxes with negative economic effects are reduced, and the overall fiscal burden not increased, it could be expected that the impact on the economy might even be *positive.* The macroeconomic advantages are likely to be twofold: (1) less environmental damage and so reduced repair and health costs; and (2) the likelihood of some increased employment because gross labour costs diminish as labour related taxes and charges are reduced.

Thus, even very high ecological taxes — provided that the principle of revenue neutrality is observed and they are introduced slowly enough — could theoretically become acceptable to both industry and society at large. During the course of several decades, it ought to be possible for such new ecological taxes to attain a level of 5-10% of GNP with other taxes being correspondingly reduced. This is indicated in Fig. 3, where the estimated levels attainable by ecological taxes are contrasted with those for other environmental economic measures, such as earmarked charges and charge-benefit systems, with much less potential and hence a much less powerful steering import on the economy.

For environmentalists, the claim that ecological taxes could bring in as much as 5-10% of GNP without damaging the economy as a whole would by itself be sufficient grounds for introducing an ecological tax reform. However, before the idea of embarking on such a programme of major social reorganisation can even be seriously considered, credible answers to a number of questions affecting both the economic and political spheres will have to be provided. For example:

- What level, or what order of magnitude, of ecological taxation can be justified in terms of *the polluter-pays-principle,* even

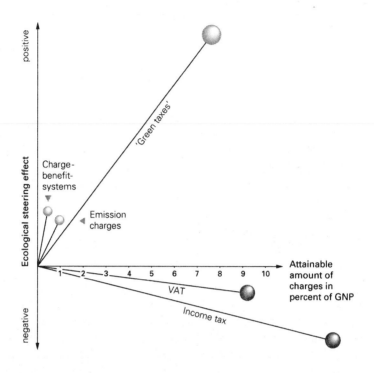

**Fig. 3:** The ecological steering effectiveness of three different charge systems. The steering effect is symbolised by the height above the horizontal line. *Specific* steering power (steering effect per dollar of charges) is symbolised by the angle of the line between zero and the relevant instruments; it is assumed to be highest with charge-benefit systems and lowest with ecological taxes. But the ultimate steering effect of ecological taxes can nevertheless significantly outstrip that of the other charge systems if they are raised in a revenue-neutral manner and are thus able to attain an amount many times higher than that obtainable through steering charges. The ecological steering effectiveness of ecological taxes will be further increased if taxes with a negative ecological steering impact are reduced. [14]

accepting that evidence of the precise origin of pollution or other ecological damage is not required?

- Does raising the cost of resource consumption have the desired steering effect? And at what level is the steering effect relatively optimum?

- What is the optimum pace for introducing such reforms?

- To fulfill the requirement of revenue neutrality, which other taxes could best be lowered?

- How can undesired distribution effects be avoided or compensated for?

This study seeks merely to provide initial answers to these questions. The whole point of this short book is to point us in a new, but practical, direction for the solution of some of our planet's most grave environmental problems, and to urge rapid and more thorough investigation of the potential, as well as the problems, of an ecological tax reform such as we propose.

## Cutting Subsidies

In addition, along with these three important economic instruments just discussed, mention should be made of the ecologically motivated reduction of state subsidies. For decades, in practically every country in the world, the consumption of electricity, coal, water and other ecologically relevant goods has been subsidised, with the state-run economies of Eastern Europe providing the most crass examples. Energy and water were ridiculously cheap, in some cases literally free, in Eastern Europe. The same is true for some of the socialist developing countries.

But OECD countries are also not without sin. Aluminium smelters and other energy-intensive industries obtain major price concessions from the mostly state-controlled power stations in many OECD countries (the Japanese were the first to stop this macroeconomic nonsense). Nearly all countries give generous subsidies or tax breaks to car commuters, under the outdated philosophy that higher commuting costs should be honoured with higher subsidies. This has made it virtually impossible for the public transport system, which is so much more energy efficient, to maintain economic competitiveness. As a result, tragically, the only steering forces that are left, are road congestion and limited parking space, which clearly is a very inefficient method of allocation leading to enormous macroeconomic losses. Another huge field of economically unjustified subsidies is agriculture, athough here the most eye-catching phenomenon is the strange system of farm price guarantees. But there are also various mechanisms to encourage excessive use of energy, for example for heavy machinery on the farm.

In general, one can say that public subsidies may have given some momentary relief to social problems but they have failed to attain their long-range socio-economic goals. They have placed a heavy burden on the entire economy and have slowed the pace of technological development. And they have had a negative, in some cases devastating, effect on the environment.

In harmonising ecological and economic goals, the dismantling of ecologically unreasonable subsidies should receive top priority. It is a basic premise of this little book that subsidies on energy and other resources involved should be removed before taxes are additionally placed on them. A step-by-step process of ecological tax reform featuring long-term predictability (see Chapters 7 and 10 in particular) likewise serves as a valid argument for dismantling subsidies.

# 4.  The Polluter Pays Principle and External Costs

The polluter pays principle is the chief economic pillar of a market-oriented environmental policy. Economic theory suggests that the common good of society as a whole is served by the successsful implementation of the polluter pays principle, i.e. when polluters are made to bear the costs of making good the damage they have inflicted. If the relative cost of avoiding damage in the first place is lower than the cost of subsequent repair, polluters will prefer to avoid causing damage.

In a host of cases, the polluter pays principle cannot be applied in any strict sense because either repair is impossible (e.g. in the case of species extinction), or the damage is nearly impossible to quantify (e.g. damage as a result of an enhanced greenhouse effect), or it is impossible to apportion legal responsibility for pollution (e.g. when committed by companies which no longer exist.)

And in many instances, pollution and causal chains are hypothetical and controversial. But for both ethical and common-sense reasons, holding out until certainty is established is simply not an option. For all these reasons, the scope for implementing the polluter pays principle in its original sense is really very limited.

From the very beginning, incidentally, this was recognised by classical environmental policy. This is why, instead of assigning clean-up costs, specific standards were established with which polluters had to comply. The expense of compliance with these standards was to be borne by the polluter, which resulted in these measures being incorrectly referred to as the 'fulfillment of the polluter pays principle'. But obviously, as already stated in the introductory chapter, this policy could not bring an end to the ecological crisis. Enormous damage is still occurring for which either no one pays, or which is paid for by all of us — the common burden principle. In both instances, the polluter pays principle is violated. Polluters shift costs 'outwards'. External costs emerge.

Quantifying external costs is not, to be sure, significantly any easier than implementing the polluter pays principle. An important starting point has been selected by Lutz Wicke [15] and many other authors, namely the inclusion of the damage resulting from the manifest reduction in the quality of life, which is in turn quantified in a willingness to pay analysis. Here, those questioned are asked how much they would be willing to pay for a certain improvement to, and/or non-deterioration of, the environment. For West Germany, Wicke arrived at total external costs something in the order of DM100 billion per annum, representing roughly 5% of the West German GNP at the time. Wicke limited his enquiry to the classic factors of air, water and soil pollution, and noise. If one were to include the more hard-to-quantify factors of climate change, loss of biological diversity, exported damage (i.e. the destruction of rain forests in the interest of debt servicing or in meeting European requirements for timber, minerals and animal feed), external costs (which becomes a euphemism for damage) of DM200 billion or 10% of GNP appear to be a more likely true estimate — and that is just for West Germany.

Compared to the figure of DM200 billion, the DM20-30 billion annually paid by polluters seems quite modest. Fig. 4 graphically illustrates this relationship.

However, one methodological or legal problem of any willingness to pay analysis ought not to be overlooked. Even if a certain segment of the population declares its willingness to pay for a better environment, it does not automatically mean that there is a corresponding willingness to make sacrifices in reality,

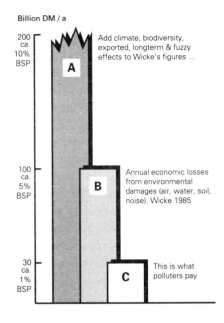

Billion DM / a

200 ca. 10% BSP

A — Add climate, biodiversity, exported, longterm & fuzzy effects to Wicke's figures ...

100 ca. 5% BSP

B — Annual economic losses from environmental damages (air, water, soil, noise). Wicke 1985

30 ca. 1% BSP

C — This is what polluters pay

**Fig. 4**: External costs due to environmental damage.
A: Estimate of total damage including long-term, exported, and 'aesthetic' damage calculated on a per annum basis for West Germany in 1985.
B: The pollution-related external costs of environmental damage (1985) according to Lutz Wicke.[15]
C: Actual costs borne by polluters in 1988.
The amounts A and B contain nominal values and should not be misconstrued as representing costs in an expenses budget sense.[16]

and certainly it does not mean that there is a willingness to pay on the part of the polluter. An ecological tax reform that would place a burden on polluters many times greater than today's could be perceived by them as quantitatively unjust, even though the polluter pays principle per se is thoroughly accepted. This is a problem to which we shall return in Chapter 8.

This perception of injustice, however, does not affect the validity of the general economic notion that an internalisation of external costs through ecological taxes is, in principle, efficient and could have a positive impact on prosperity.

Already in 1920, the British economist Arthur Cecil Pigou[17] suggested that, in order to bring macro- and micro-economic goals closer together, factors that produce external costs should be subjected to taxation. If a 'Pigou tax' were to be imposed, the cost would be incorporated into managerial calculations (i.e. internalised) and micro- and macro-economic goals would become one and the same.

In the presence of external effects, Pigou taxes can be seen as a constituent element of an ideal market economy. For the most important group of external effects, environmental problems, Pigou taxes can be introduced in actual market economies in the form of ecological taxes. In accordance with the considerations mentioned above, an amount totalling some 5-10% of GNP could be justified.

However, it must be borne in mind that, with the gigantic amount of 5-10% of GNP, changes in costs would ruin the profitability of entire industries and result in very high adjustment costs for broad sections of society. Such radical changes would in turn result in very high social costs. A Pigou-type tax reform that clings dogmatically to the polluter pays principle and ignores the resulting social costs would, from the standpoint of economic theory, be anything but the optimum one.

Obviously, it is a matter of introducing, smoothly and in a way that avoids a social uproar, a condition where external ecological costs are largely avoided. After all, the goal is to set in motion the *process* of a reorientation towards environmentally and climatically benign ways of production and consumption.

Technological change, as the most important component of the impact of ecological taxes, is not guided by short-term costs alone, but rather more by the mid- and long-term expectations of companies. Not only for social reasons but also for technological ones, therefore, the certain expectation of high raw material and energy prices in ten, twenty or thirty years is preferable to a brutal initial tax increase with an outcome that would in any case be uncertain in both economic and political terms. This is why one essential characteristic of the ecological tax reform we propose assumes that it be introduced in a steady and predictable manner over a period of several decades.

# 5.   The Importance of Price Elasticity

The next question to be asked is that of steering effectiveness. Even if an ecological tax reform is morally and theoretically justified, the question remains as to whether it will have the desired effect in practice.

In casual political discussion, the question is normally posed and answered in 'static' terms. How will the car user, for example, change his or her behaviour to reduce petrol consumption in reaction to a certain price increase? Or, in more scientific terms, what is the short-term price elasticity for petrol consumption or for any other product?

In reality, static or immediate elasticity is *systematically* much lower than dynamic, long-term elasticity. And the elasticity in response to a short-term price change is systematically lower than with a sustained, calculable price increase over a longer period.

To clarify and illustrate the reasons for the discrepancy between short- and long-term elasticities, we may distinguish five consecutive phases of adjustment to higher prices. The energy price movements in the 1970s seem to provide a good empirical background. They were characterised by a shock-like price signal large enough to be noticed by everyone and to elicit immediate reactions.

- The *first stage* of adjustment:
The consumer tries to get by on less energy. Hot water is no longer allowed to flow needlessly down the drain, windows are closed in winter and roller-shutters let down at night. Driving at top speed on highways, and senseless accelerating in suburban traffic will be reduced or avoided. Also, a number of minor

sacrifices occur, e.g. dispensing with certain weekend trips by car, lowering the thermostat on the central heating and doing without oil-heating for swimming pools.

This stage of adjustment affects energy consumption with practically no delay; however, the effects are limited (approximately 10-20% during the second oil crisis of 1979-80).

• The *second stage* of adjustment:

The criterion of energy efficiency becomes more important when purchasing energy-dependent goods (cars, household appliances) and systems (heating). Fuel consumption in cars plays a role again. This process is also reflected in advertising. During the second oil crisis in 1979-80, most car advertisements emphasised fuel efficiency and explicitly provided fuel consumption data for specified speeds and conditions (90 km/h, 120 km/h, urban traffic etc). With the subsequent decline of oil prices, this sort of data largely disappeared from advertising and consumer test reports.

This stage of adjustment takes effect gradually and the full impact is attained only when all goods are replaced by more efficient ones.

• The *third stage* of adjustment:

Suppliers of energy consuming goods respond to the change in demand structure by *developing* more efficient types. In the construction sector, this means the development of more efficient heating systems for houses and office blocks and the reduction in heating requirements through more efficient insulation, control and air circulation systems. With cars, we could expect the further development of more fuel efficient diesel and Otto engines, as well as a reduction in wind resistance, tyre friction and vehicle weight.

After running for a period of several years, this stage of adjustment produces distinctly tangible results. For instance, the low air resistance values of today's cars are the result of development efforts made in reaction to the high fuel costs during the oil crisis of 1979-80.

• The *fourth stage* of adjustment:
The state and producers of energy consuming goods invest in the *research and development of energy efficient systems* and in technologies which are able to make do without fossil (and nuclear) energy. Examples of this would be innovative insulation and energy saving recycling systems, heat pumps, unconventional engines for cars (Stirling engines, gas turbines, fuel cells), quick and efficient public transport systems with the requisite expansion of infrastructure, and finally the development of renewable energy sources.

This stage of adjustment attains its full impact only after an extended period (perhaps 10-40 years), owing to the slowness of infrastructural changes and new technological developments, although certain results of research that already exist could go into serial production much earlier.

• The *fifth stage* of adjustment:
Demand for energy decreases due to changes in the *housing structure*, the *infrastructure* and the general *way of life* (culture, in the broadest sense of the word). For instance, the average distance between home and the work place could be reduced, leisure facilities could be relocated to locations closer to residential areas, and greenfield site shopping centres could be abandoned in favour of decentralised neighbourhood stores. Long-distance road freight transport and the greater part of passenger-traffic could be shifted on to the by now more efficient rail and other mass transit systems.

The full impact of this stage of adjustment will only emerge during the course of several decades.

The boundaries between each stage of adjustment are not clearly defined. It is important to acknowledge that the higher stages require time. This is the reason why price-demand elasticities using short-term data only provide a false impression. [18]

A proper determination of the price-demand elasticity of energy could theoretically be made if all of the above listed stages of adjustment were included, in particular if the high fuel price period of the late 1970s had extended over several decades. However, during this period, other relevant variables would also change (e.g. per capita income, population density, and scientific and technical progress) which, in turn, would render causal analysis more difficult.

However, a measure useful in determining what long-term price elasticity might be should be obtainable if price differences had existed over longer periods for certain identical or comparable goods in *different* countries with comparable economies. In this case, specific consumption differences for such goods could be correlated to the different prices. In doing so, the influence of other variables must, of course, be considered but should be able to be separated from the price elasticity calculation.

In the next chapter, an example of a model for this will be discussed. The analysis is inevitably rather technical and readers, so inclined, are invited to move straight to Chapter 7. The important point to note is that there are good empirical grounds for concluding that there can be a very high price elasticity for a raw material — the example we investigate in the next chapter is fossil fuel which both damages the environment in the short term and is likely to be in short supply in the long term — if prices rise steadily and significantly over a period of many years. This is where an ecological tax reform — in this case, sustained energy price rises as a result of rising taxes — can intervene in the market place with the reliable expectation that it will have a major impact on economic behaviour, steering it into more benign resource and environment-friendly patterns.

# 6. Price Elasticity for Fuels: A New Measurement Concept

## Elasticity in the Past

In the search for appropriate goods, and for goods which are relevant to the ecological tax debate, one quickly encounters petrol and diesel fuel used by road vehicles of all types. These have been very heavily taxed in Japan and Italy, heavily but differently taxed in other West European countries, and hardly taxed at all in North America. They thus lend themselves to an initial assessment of long-term price elasticities better than virtually any other group of goods, and in an area of utmost relevance to environmental policy.

On the one hand, the purpose of such an assessment is to gain an indication as to how high ecological taxes would have to be in order to guarantee that the necessary ecological goals are successfully met. On the other hand, the assessment can provide an idea of the distribution effects caused by ecological taxes, and thus of what need may exist for compensation measures.

Based on 1985 energy prices, we have conducted an initial analysis of the connection between the level of fuel prices and per capita fuel consumption in the most important OECD countries. It indicates — with just these two variables being employed — the existence of a high negative correlation, as is illustrated in Fig. 5.

The residual variance in relation to the regression line in the figure is remarkably low. The correlation coefficient amounts to -0.93. This very high correlation may in part be due to coincidence, in part also to third factors correlating positively with fuel consumption and negatively with fuel prices. One such possible factor is low population density which makes average

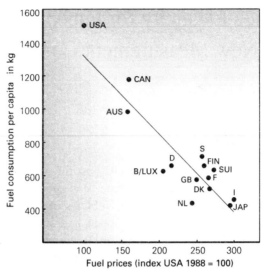

**Fig. 5:** Fuel prices and per capita consumption in the most important OECD countries, with letter-symbols corresponding to the standard abbreviations for the countries involved.

distances longer and may make fuel taxation politically much more sensitive than in densely populated countries. We shall discuss this factor below. In a purely statistical sense, however, the negative correlation between price and per capita consumption is very well established.

The relationship shown in Fig. 5 should make us cautious about the widespread belief that the problem of fuel consumption can be dealt with effectively by the adoption of fuel efficiency standards. As is well known, the United States introduced car fleet efficiency standards in the mid-1970s. The graph shows that, even after more than ten years, these standards failed to pull the USA below the regression line. Some further reflection may offer an explanation for this failure. Fuel efficiency standards have no restrictive influence on the number of kilometres driven. Quite the contrary. At constant fuel prices they actually make more kilometres affordable to car owners. The best that can be said for the US's fuel efficiency standards is that without them,

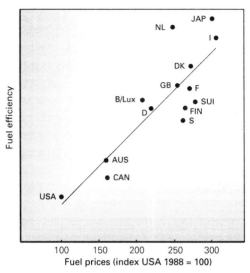

**Fig. 6:** 1988 fuel prices and macro-economic fuel efficiency in the most important OECD countries.

the United States would probably be *even* worse off in terms of international comparison.

By its very nature, the straight line in Fig. 5 cannot realistically be extrapolated for higher fuel prices. This is because fuel prices that were only about a third higher than the Italian-Japanese level would result in negative fuel consumption rates. An asymptotic approach towards the zero line would instead seem plausible. A simple mathematical transformation is convenient when extrapolating the findings beyond the Japanese price level. Instead of per capita fuel consumption, we may plot its reciprocal value. The value obtained from the relationship 1/fuel consumption can be called macro-economic fuel efficiency (or just fuel efficiency) — where there is no confusion with the technical notion of fuel efficiency applying to individual cars). Macro-economic fuel efficiency is a measure of how efficient the inhabitants of countries of similar economic performance are in their use of fuel. Fig. 6 shows the relationship between fuel efficiency in this sense and price, for the year 1988.

The higher the macro-economic fuel efficiency, the lower the specific fuel consumption. The correlation coefficient in Fig. 6 of $r = 0.85$ is not quite as high as in the previous graph. However, as opposed to the simple illustration in the first graph, even with high prices no negative consumption values appear here.

Naturally, Figures 5 and 6 provide only a view at a particular moment in time — the year 1988. For every year, slightly different but probably parallel lines would be obtained due to the fact the relevant factors, while keeping on changing, only vary rather slightly. In the following graph, Fig. 7, fuel efficiency in relation to fuel price is portrayed for the years 1980, 1982, 1984, 1987 and 1988.

It can be seen from Fig. 7 that the correlation between macro-economic fuel efficiency (as a measure of the economic use of

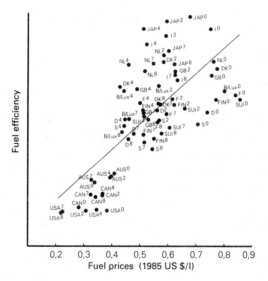

**Fig. 7:** Chronological development of fuel efficiency and fuel prices. In this pattern of chronological development, the impact of prosperity is readily apparent. The abbreviation code for each country is followed by the last digit of the respective year.

fuels) and fuel prices becomes less distinct due to dispersal during various years. The strong dispersal reflects the relatively low short-term price elasticity. However, it ought to be possible to trace some of the effect back to parameters other than price. For this reason, and because we were curious about the possible influence of other parameters, we have attempted to include in our analysis here a few other such factors.

Aside from fuel price, it is plausible that the most important variable is per capita income. In rich countries, not only is the number of cars per capita greater, they are also larger, more expensive and less economical. Taking GNP per capita as an approximate measure of the relative prosperity of a country, the result is shown in Fig 8.

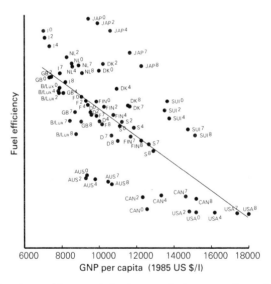

**Fig. 8:** There is a positive correlation between fuel consumption and prosperity. Correspondingly, macro-economic fuel efficiency decreases with growing prosperity. This can be read both from the chronological development within the individual countries and from the overall picture. The graph plots fuel efficiency against GNP per capita. The last digit of the years 1980, 1982, 1984, 1987 and 1988 appear after the country symbols.

The examples of Japan (J) and Italy (I), in particular, show how increasing incomes during the years 1980-88 led to falling fuel efficiency levels. To be sure, the correlation coefficient of r = -0.67 is distinctly lower than for the correlation between efficiency and fuel prices. But the incomes variable should by no means be neglected in describing the differences in fuel consumption.

A further decisive factor is population density. The more densely settled a country is, the closer will its population centres be to each other, the more elaborate will be its public transport system, and the shorter the average distances to be covered. The following graph, Fig. 9, shows the connection between fuel efficiency and population density.

It can clearly be seen that, although a correlation exists, in the short term it is not particularly conspicuous, in spite of a high correlation coefficient (r = 0.7). It is all too obvious that the

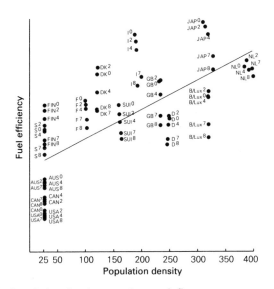

**Fig. 9:** Population density, too, has an influence on macro-economic fuel efficiency. Population density and fuel efficiency for the years 1980, 1982, 1984, 1987 and 1988 are shown here.

movements from 1980 to 1988 are diagonal to the regression line, meaning that at least in the short term, other variables (fuel price, incomes) play a dominant role. Structures influenced by population density, such as settlement patterns and the extent of public transport, hardly vary at all in the short run. However, density is a vital explanatory variable in that it obviously has a marked long-term influence. And it is not far-fetched to speculate that, in the long term, micro-regional density patterns in turn are strongly influenced by fuel prices.

The proportion of income necessary for purchasing a specific amount of fuel could also be taken into account as a further possible explanatory variable. This 'relative' fuel price, obtained by the simple division of fuel price by incomes, reveals a rather high correlation to fuel consumption, as shown in Fig. 10. At r = 0.8, the correlation is better than with the previously considered individual variables.

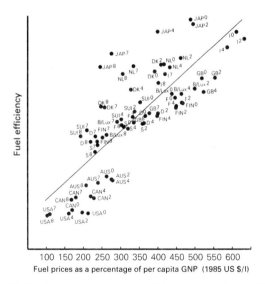

100 150 200 250 300 350 400 450 500 550 600
Fuel prices as a percentage of per capita GNP (1985 US $/l)

**Fig. 10:** Fuel prices as a percentage of income correlate well with macro-economic fuel efficiency. Here, fuel efficiency (ordinate) is contrasted with the relationship of fuel prices and per capita GNP (abscissa).

An investigation as to whether or not a still higher degree of precision and clarity could be obtained by incorporating all of the variables under consideration into a single analysis would appear to be the next logical step. Assuming that we can multiply the influences of each factor to arrive at the elasticity in dependence on all three, then fuel efficiency can be expressed as follows:

$$FE = f_1(P)\ f_2(D)\ f_3(W)$$

whereby $f_1$, $f_2$ and $f_3$ are simple exponential functions of the real fuel price P, the population density D, and 'wealth' W, measured as the real GNP per capita.[19] In the following 'mixed index', the three explanatory variables of fuel price, wealth and population density will be referred to respectively as P, W and D. The respective components have been estimated for the years under examination (1980-88). Somewhat to our surprise, a remarkably high correlation coefficient was obtained (approximately r = 0.9), provided the three variables under consideration were weighted in such a manner as to maximise the possible corre-

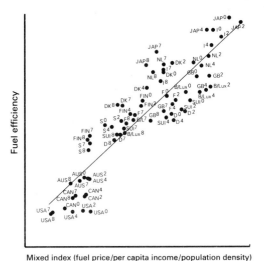

Mixed index (fuel price/per capita income/population density)

**Fig. 11:** A mixed index consisting of fuel price, per capita income and population density with optimised weighting factors features a very high correlation with macro-economic fuel efficiency.

lation. This means that, at least for the period 1980-88, per capita consumption can largely be explained by these three variables. This is shown in the following graph, Fig. 11.

This statistically well substantiated graph line in the figure can be expressed in the following equation:

*Macro-economic Fuel Efficiency*
$$FE = 221+30.6 \ (P^{0.9} \ D^{0.182} \ B^{-0.277}) \qquad (1a)$$

or, as the reciprocal of fuel efficiency:

*Fuel Consumption*
$$FC = 1000/(221+30.6 \ (P^{0.9} \ D^{0.182} \ B^{-0.277})) \quad (1b) \ \text{with:}$$

FE = macro-economic fuel efficiency
FC = per capita consumption  (in tons of fuel p.a.)
P   = price level                    (in 1985  US \$/t oil equivalent)
D   = population density        (in inhabitants per km²)
W  = per capita income          (in 1985 US \$/inhabitant). [20]

The correlation between fuel efficiency and the three variables under consideration here becomes even clearer when a single year is examined. This can be seen in Fig. 12.

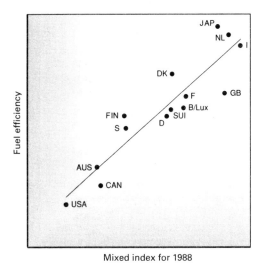

**Fig. 12:** Macro-economic fuel efficiency plotted against the mixed index of equation (1a) for 1988.

The equations (1a) and (1b), or (1) for short, represent an equilibrium state which shows the dependence of fuel consumption on the three factors. We will frequently refer to it as the empirical price elasticity of fuel consumption and/or fuel efficiency, although elements of 'wealth elasticity' and 'density elasticity' are concealed within the equation. Elasticities may be calculated as movements along the regression line. For small (i.e. marginal) price changes, the (price) elasticity is around -0.75; the respective income elasticity is +0.25. The accuracy of this simple estimate equation is in the vicinity of ± 25 %.

For 1988, the situation appears as follows (Table 1).

An 'individual factor' is given for each country. If it lies below (or over) 1, then the per capita consumption in this country is lower (or higher) than that expected from the regression analysis. This individual factor cannot be estimated, but must nevertheless be taken into account if forecasts are to be made on the basis of this equation with altered parameters.

**Table 1**

| Country | Per capita consumption according to equation (1b) | Real per capita consumption (in kg) | Deviation | Individual factor (= deviation +1.0) |
|---------|------|------|------|------|
| AUS | 985 | 981 | 0.4 % | 0.996 |
| B/Lux* | 623 | 624 | 0.2 % | 1.002 |
| CAN | 964 | 1175 | 22 % | 1.220 |
| DK | 655 | 518 | 20.9 % | 0.791 |
| FIN | 833 | 656 | 21.3 % | 0.787 |
| F | 617 | 584 | 5.3 % | 0.947 |
| D | 672 | 657 | 2.1 % | 0.979 |
| I | 502 | 454 | 9.5 % | 0.905 |
| JAP | 544 | 419 | 23.1 % | 0.769 |
| NL | 523 | 433 | 17.1 % | 0.829 |
| S | 826 | 712 | 13.8 % | 0.862 |
| SUI | 659 | 631 | 4.2 % | 0.958 |
| GB | 531 | 573 | 8.1 % | 1.081 |
| USA | 1254 | 1498 | 19.7 % | 1.197 |

* Belgium and Luxembourg taken together

## A 'Retro-Prognosis'

With the help of the elasticity equation (1) it is also possible to carry out a sort of retro-prognosis — i.e. calculating what the level of equilibrium per capita consumption of fuel could have been expected at different prices, if different prices had determined the behaviour of car owners, automobile producers and transport policy-makers over the decades. By way of example, let's examine what per capita consumption would have looked like if all countries had had (1) Canadian, (2) German and (3) Italian price levels, as well as the presumed levels of consumption at an increased price of US $1,500 per ton of oil equivalent, which roughly corresponds to three Deutschmarks per litre (or one pound sterling, or getting on for two US dollars per litre). The result is contained in Table 2.

**Table 2:** According to equation (1), over the course of time the various countries would have experienced a per capita fuel consumption different from those they actually experienced.

| Country | Density | GNP per capita | Individual factor from Table 1 | Current consumption | Hypothetical consumption at a persistent price level according to that of: | | |
|---|---|---|---|---|---|---|---|
| | | | | | CAN | I | 1500$/t |
| AUS | 25.0 | 10630 | 0.996 | 981 | 975 | 614 | 376 |
| B/Lux* | 317.8 | 8715 | 1.002 | 624 | 754 | 464 | 280 |
| CAN | 25.0 | 15140 | 1.219 | *1175* | *1175* | 738 | 452 |
| DK | 119.1 | 11510 | 0.791 | 518 | 755 | 474 | 290 |
| FIN | 25.0 | 12200 | 0.788 | 656 | 920 | 591 | 367 |
| F | 101.1 | 10110 | 0.947 | 584 | 851 | 532 | 324 |
| D | 244.3 | 10950 | 0.978 | *657* | 822 | 510 | 310 |
| I | 191.2 | 8133 | 0.904 | *454* | 733 | *454* | 275 |
| JAP | 325.8 | 12210 | 0.770 | 419 | 665 | 414 | 251 |
| NL | 397.8 | 9032 | 0.828 | 433 | 599 | 368 | 221 |
| S | 25.0 | 12850 | 0.862 | 712 | 991 | 636 | 394 |
| SUI | 161.6 | 15080 | 0.958 | 631 | 933 | 587 | 359 |
| GB | 232.1 | 8984 | 1.079 | 573 | 806 | 496 | 299 |
| USA | 25.0 | 17970 | 1.197 | 1498 | 1096 | 685 | 418 |

* Belgium and Luxembourg taken together

We see, for instance, that in the United States fuel consumption would have been 25% less if, over a long period of time, it had had the same price level as neighbouring Canada. At a uniform price level of $1,500 per ton, the US would have consumed only 395 kg per capita per annum, and the Netherlands (due to its higher population density and lower per capita income) only 196 kg per capita per annum.

Obviously, this is a hypothetical *ex post facto* analysis. More relevant is the question whether the estimate can be applied to the future.

**Valid for the Future?**

This 'retro-prognosis' will satisfy neither practical nor policy concerns. More important is an elasticity estimate for the future. It must first be stated that at least four factors make using our empirical elasticity model for predicting the future difficult:

1) With a uniform price level for oil in the OECD countries and elsewhere, automobile manufacturers would be confronted with an entirely novel market situation. While economical vehicles were previously designed only for specific countries (e.g. Japan and Italy), the very large US market would also now be of interest to producers of such vehicles. In other words, if fuel prices were as high in the US as they already are in Italy, consumption levels would probably also be lower in Italy, since the development of energy saving vehicles would not have been limited to the Italian market. The estimate is thus rather conservative, meaning that the anticipated decline in consumption might (due to economies of scale) actually be greater.

2) The analysis assumes per capita income and population density at current levels. In the case of population density, this is not critical, since it will barely change in the industrialised countries. Real incomes, however, usually climb several percentage points each year. This must be taken account of in the interpretation process. Forecasts must include anticipated rises in

annual per capita income, and savings in forecast energy usage (with unchanged fuel prices) must be seen in relation to the expected trend. Assuming a real GNP growth of 2% per annum, fuel consumption in the US for the $1500/ton case we are looking at by way of example would in any case be almost 6% higher in 20 years' time than if incomes had remained unchanged. From this standpoint, the estimate is thus overly optimistic.

3) There could be some element of an autonomous consumption trend. This is, in the nature of things, difficult to prove, since there has never been a long period of constant fuel prices, incomes and population density. Here, too, calculated savings must be seen in relation to this (hypothetical) trend.

4) If the price of fuel increased to such a degree that biofuels, solar-powered cars and other non-fossil fuels became competitive, the consumption of fossil fuels would drop much more quickly than is indicated by historically based elasticity estimates. In this respect, too, the estimate is therefore overly conservative.

# 7. What Would Happen If There Were a Significant Annual Increase in Fuel Prices?

### Extrapolation from the Empirically Derived Elasticity of Macro-economic Fuel Efficiency

The empirical results of the OECD country comparison of fuel efficiency in the previous chapter may be used as the basis for a consideration of the future, in other words for a scenario. Let us assume in this scenario that prices for petroleum-based fuels will increase by 5% to 7% per annum. The average total tax 'take' or burden is to remain constant, and a continued increase in prosperity is also assumed.

The elasticity equation (1) developed in Chapter 6 indicates what per capita fuel consumption would have been if the underlying factors (i.e. price, average incomes and population density) had remained constant over a period of several decades. Because the time lags inherent in the system are not taken into consideration, the results obtained with the equation are more or less useless for short-term forecasting of changes in fuel consumption.

The process of adjustment to new circumstances (higher fuel prices, higher incomes) in part proceeds quickly (for example, more economical driving practices, or switching to bicycles and public transport), and in part very slowly. It takes nearly a decade to develop and bring on to the market a new automobile. It will take even longer to develop and establish an entirely new infrastructure adapted to higher fuel prices.

Similar considerations apply to the adjustment of the 'objective' demand for transport to new circumstances. Thus, the distance between home and office (an indicator of demand for

44

commuter tranportation) will diminish only very gradually; the speed of this adjustment will depend on the one hand on the normal rate of change in places of residence and workplace, and on the other, on the pressure to adjust. Someone who has built a house in the distant suburbs is unlikely to sell it in order to be closer to his place of employment unless the price pressure of commuting is very great. Companies which have invested in just-in-time concepts will only slowly return to a division of labour that requires less transport.

In part, these processes of adjustment proceed so imperceptibly slowly that they cannot be registered using traditional methods of analysis. Measurement of price and income elasticities over longer periods of time (usually carried out with the help of national data) are thus systematically too low — even when the label of long-term elasticity is applied to them. Only a cross-section analysis of several countries, such as we have carried out, will be able to reflect the situation which will exist at the close of the adjustment process.

Turning to the ecological aspects, the equilibrium values are highly interesting. This is because the strength of the greenhouse effect is the result (to the extent that it is due to $CO_2$) of the cumulative entry of $CO_2$ into the atmosphere over the course of several decades. Rather than quick successes, it is a sustainable and strong reduction in the amount of $CO_2$ entering the atmosphere that is the goal from the ecological standpoint. Whether a new equilibrium level of fuel consumption at a lower threshold is reached today, or not until 20 years from now, although ecologically speaking not unimportant, is not really decisive.

In contrast to this, with regard to both the political and economic aspects, it is above all the short- and medium-term aspects which are relevant. The normal range of vision of politicians, entrepreneurs or motorists simply does not extend 20 years. Instead they want to know what the impact of a fuel price increase is going to be today or during the next two or three years. In order to satisfy the curiosity of a finance minister (with his or her interest in tax revenue) and of the motorist (concerned with the cost of petrol), it is necessary that we embark on the elaborate course of simulating a society's adjustment to higher fuel prices.

## A System Dynamics Simulation

System dynamics is a procedure for simulating dynamic processes. It became well known internationally through the World Model of Jay Forrester and the Meadows, the results of which were published in *Limits to Growth* (see note 7). It describes complex interactions by means of a period-related incremental method which is especially suitable for those processes where the interactive influence of the variables is difficult to describe mathematically.

We have drawn up a simple system dynamics model to simulate the process of adjustment to the imposition of new ecological taxes. In principle, the model is suitable for most green taxes, although up until now it has been implemented and tested only for car fuels (petrol and diesel). The basic assumptions of the model are as follows:

- There is a long-term equilibrium for the most important OECD countries between the exogenous variables of fuel price, per capita GNP and population density and the per capita consumption of fuel, which was determined by using the methods of regression analysis and used as the basis for the calculation of this model.

- In the long run, a new equilibrium will be reached as long as the three exogenous variables can be held constant over a long period of time, i.e. several decades.

- Adjustments will proceed depending on the level and rate of change of these three variables.

Within the model the speed and nature of the adjustment processes will in the short and medium term be determined by the following factors:

(i) The difference between the actual and equilibrium level of consumption. It is assumed in the model that the greater the difference, the higher the adjustment pressure will be. So this inter-relationship is non-linear.

(ii) Price expectations of consumers and producers are based on past experience. This pattern in shifts in price expectations is assumed because of our experience of the 1970s oil crises, when car producers, expecting a continuation of the upward trend in fuel prices, invested in new technologies (e.g. wind tunnel measurements of air resistance) to a degree that cannot be explained by the level of oil prices *per se*.

(iii) Quasi-constants such as the average length of time required to develop and introduce new technologies to the market. 'Quasi' because even these factors are adjusted within the model to changes in the exogenous variables. Thus, for instance, it can be expected that the scrapping of old vehicles (as a measure of the speed at which more fuel efficient new vehicles are entering the market), will be more pronounced, the greater is the difference between the 'market-worthiness' (in terms of dependence on fuel prices and perhaps other factors) of old and new vehicles.

Many of the required fixed parameters inherent in the model (e.g. the reaction of car buyers and the R&D activities of automobile manufacturers, depending on the degree of pressure to adjust) are unknown and have thus had to be estimated.

In order to avoid arbitrary estimates for such parameters, we have chosen the elaborate, but in our view effective, way of calibrating the model by using past data. The time-frame selected for comparison was the decade of the 1980s, a period which was characterised by major fluctuations in the price of oil.

The parameters of the model were initially set at a starting value on the basis of certain plausibility assumptions. Then all of the necessary parameters were adjusted so that discrepancies between the per capita consumption values calculated within the model and the actual consumption values were minimised even for the short term.

After multiple runs using this method, the divergences from reality within the model could be reduced to (at most) a few percentage points. Thus, we seem to have succeeded in finding a method which is sufficiently precise with respect to both short- and medium-term adjustments and long-term results.

The applicability to the future of results obtained with the assistance of empirical data from the recent past can — with certain limitations discussed in Chapter 7 — be assumed to be good. In contrast to the now infamous official predictions of the 1970s, we have not limited ourselves to simply extrapolating trends. Rather, it can be concluded from our country-specific calibration in Chapter 6 that the most important factors have been incorporated in the model. Only such variables as population density, income or politically determined fuel costs, which must be seen as being externally determined, are defined in the model as exogenous.

Theoretically, it cannot be ruled out that an intensive change in value perceptions could alter consumer behaviour to such a degree that the equilibrium equation would lose its validity. However, it must be borne in mind that the equilibrium equation is built on the past consumer behaviour of a half a billion people. It seems somewhat unlikely that the behaviour of such a large percentage of the Earth's population would all of a sudden no longer be based on price, income and utility considerations, but instead on idealistic concerns. This hypothesis is also supported by the fact that even during the oil crisis, a phase featuring a very high — indeed, almost hysterical — level of public awareness of the need to husband resources (car-free Sundays in some countries!), no great changes in behaviour were to be observed which could not be ascribed to higher fuel prices. 'I'm an energy saver' bumper stickers, which in those days could be seen on compacts and luxury limousines alike, are no substitute for actually doing without a car. In light of these actual experiences, we do not assume that the consumption of petroleum used for transportation will be reduced to any significant degree as a result of idealistic, non-economic and non-compulsory influences.

Below, we show several examples of the results attained using this model. Presented in the following four graphs is the development of fuel prices, fuel consumption and tax revenue in accordance with the elasticity equation (1) during a 30 year tax reform period in which account is taken of the above mentioned system inertia.

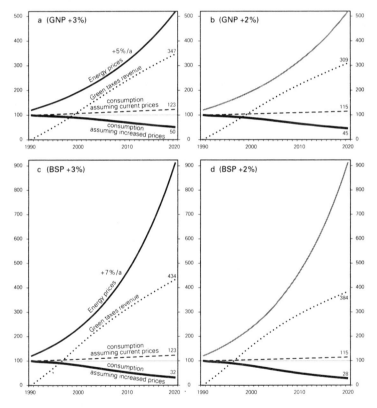

**Fig. 13 a/b and c/d:** Reductions in fuel consumption as a result of fuel taxes — and resulting tax revenue — calculated according to the empirically derived elasticity equation (1) with four different assumptions concerning the annual increase in fuel prices and gross national product (in real terms).

## The Possibilities of Even More Dramatic Changes

The price elasticities we have demonstrated to exist in all likelihood represent an — albeit carefully calibrated — extrapolation of the actual dependence of fuel consumption on price and prosperity as observed during the 1980s. It is, however, not only possible but even likely that elasticity will increase markedly yet again as certain threshold price levels are exceeded. Of particular interest is the price level at which — for the first time since the automobile became a means of mass transport — non-fossil fuels become competitive. Whereas the whole of the empirically demonstrated elasticity of the 1980s resulted from the worldwide circumstance that petroleum was the sole available basis for fuels (with alternative engines and fuels being used only experimentally or in isolated special cases), a doubling of petrol and diesel prices would certainly mean the entry into the market of bio-fuel (fuel obtained from renewable sources). And with even higher petroleum prices, as well as an ecologically motivated increase in the cost of bio-fuel through taxation, solar energy and hydrogen would finally break into the market.

Substitution may already be just around the corner, considering the decreasing costs for renewables. The US Department of Energy has made a cost comparison of various energy sources for the production of electricity. It is reproduced in Fig. 14.

It can be seen here that — as far as the US situation is concerned — fuels derived from renewable resources in fact now cost considerably less than twice the price of petroleum.

In the opening section of this chapter we assumed that in the period of the first doubling of fuel prices (which would be about within about 10 years with a 7% increase per annum, or within 14 years with a 5% increase per annum), the most important effect of the price increase would be the introduction of more fuel efficient automobiles. If, then, it is further assumed that during the same initial period a certain proportion of the fuel supply will be drawn from renewable sources, this will function as an additional impetus for a reduction in petroleum consumption,

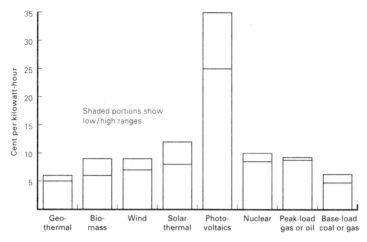

**Fig. 14 :** Even today the difference in price between petroleum and plant-derived fuel is no longer all that great. The bars show the current price per kilowatt hour for the electricty market. Source: US Dept. of Energy.[21]

and hence $CO_2$ emissions. With a predictable trend of ever increasing petroleum prices, agriculture and forestry will move at an early stage in order to be able to make plant-based fuels available.

After a further period of petroleum price doubling (even allowing for a general increase in prosperity), petrol consumption would continue to drop off drastically; hardly a single new car that was completely dependent on petroleum would be registered in the countries carrying out the ecological tax reform on fossil fuels. Petrol consumption for transportation would then become limited to older cars and to visitors from countries with low petroleum prices.

Already during the first period in which petrol prices doubled, a massive replanning of freight traffic would have to take place. Industry and government agencies responsible for infrastructure would have to get used to the idea that transporting freight by road would grow more expensive every year. This is because fuel efficiency for heavy goods vehicles and trucks cannot be improved to the same extent as with cars. An extension and modernisation of the rail network, shipping facilities and local distribution systems could become the order of the day. The extension and modernisation of these environmentally more sustainable transport systems would be possible both technically and economically. But the changes involved require a great deal of time. Thus, it cannot be expected that a major reduction in road traffic — whether it be passenger vehicles or lorries — will occur during the first decade of the process.

In contrast, during the *second* period in which prices for fuel doubled, a massive shift of freight transport over to rail and waterways is to be expected. To be sure, this effect is presumably already taken into partial account in the empirically based elasticity equation of Chapter 6. During the decades of the (American) trucking boom, in countries with higher fuel prices, railroads, inland waterways and coastal shipping were able to hold their own better than in those countries with lower fuel prices. However, a further increase in fuel savings during the second doubling period (10–14 years) can be expected if, for the first time in history, technological development, with both public and private sector investment, is consistently dedicated over a period of many years to the task of organising the transport of freight along new lines.

A further factor which has become utterly irrelevant in the modern history of mobility — and was thus not included in the elasticity equation in Chapter 6 — is power derived from the sun, water, wind and muscle. In past centuries, the horse and cart and the sailing ship were the most important technical means of transport. For more than 50 years now they have been economically irrelevant in the industrialised countries. But with predictably rising prices for petroleum, a revival of these environmentally sustainable power sources is a foregone conclusion. Indeed, although this time on a high-tech level, the sailing ship could experience a renaissance. New high-tech materials and new control systems could render the sailing ship the ideal means of transporting goods over very long distances in situations where speed is not a critical factor.

The bicycle is also sure to take on increased significance again. In order to be a viable alternative to the car for longer distance as well, buses and trains will have to be designed to allow passengers to take their bicycles with them (naturally not cost-free). Also, the construction of theft-proof bicycle storage racks and perhaps even covered bicycle paths, the introduction of environmentally friendly auxiliary motors for going uphill (like the bike invented by Sinclair in Britain in 1991 and already commercially available), and the development of new baggage racks, new gear shifting systems, along with a host of other innovations, could combine to make the bicycle a highly attractive vehicle for many cities and villages.

Cars powered by hydrogen produced in plants located away from ecologically sensitive areas could also become competitive without difficultyonce carbon-based fuels become priced at some-what more than one pound sterling (or some two US dollars) per litre, particularly if local clean air regulations (as in California) were to begin pushing the classic internal combustion engine off the market. Also, combinations consisting of batteries, solar power and conventional fuels could significantly influence or even dominate the market within the next one or two decades.[22]

The number and the effect on traffic of possible high-tech innovations for an environmentally sustainable mobility is very great. It is no more possible to make a detailed forecast of the effect of rising petroleum (and bio-fuel) prices on transport developments than it would have been in 1965 to have forecast the development and scope of application of micro-electronics over the following 30 years. But, given the introduction of a tax on fossil fuels of the kind we are advocating, we may certainly reckon on a dramatic reduction in petrol consumption in three decades, even if mobility is not limited by this. Once petroleum prices have risen eight-fold, not much petrol would be sold at the filling pumps — presuming the system is given sufficient time to develop alternatives.

Figure 15 (next page) shows how fuel sales and engine systems could develop over the course of 42 years (three doubling periods) given a yearly 5% rate of increase in the petroleum price in real terms, and, starting in the second doubling period, an annual increase of 2.5% in real terms in the price of bio-fuel.

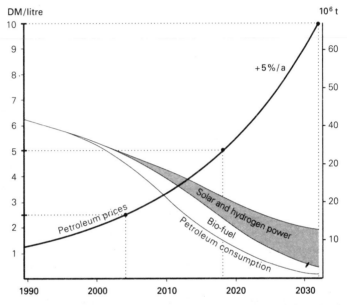

**Fig. 15:** The approximate (and inevitably to some degree speculative) development of fuel sales and the success of solar and hydrogen powered cars under the assumption of an annual 5% increase in petroleum prices, as well as an annual 2.5% increase in the price of bio-fuel (the latter commencing in the second period of doubling petroleum prices).

The figure shows impressively — though inevitably to some degree speculatively — how a virtually complete phasing out of petroleum for use in motor transport could be achieved within the relatively brief time span of 40 years. Especially noteworthy here is the fact that motor transport is generally viewed today as being the one area where long-term progress in containing greenhouse gases seems virtually hopeless.

An acceleration of the phasing out process could doubtless be attained by raising the petroleum prices by 7% per annum in real terms (i.e. a doubling of prices in ten years). But in view of the dramatic adjustment reactions already anticipated for the 5% rate, this does not even seem necessary.

The not so desirable side of the remarkable efficiency of an ecological tax reform is that tax revenues from this source would remain far below that assumed in Fig. 13 a-d and could fall away completely in the foreseeable future.

During the second decade of the process, at the latest, for reasons of nature conservancy or on account of competition for land for agriculture, reservations concerning, and resistance to, a further expansion of so-called fuel plantations will be encountered. Concerns would also be voiced about how these bio-fuel plantations would be fertilised, due to the related production of $N_2O$ which is also a very persistent and very 'efficient' greenhouse gas. Thus, aside from regulatory measures (the designation of nature protection areas, safeguarding land-use variety, and restrictions on the use of chemicals), the introduction of taxes on bio-fuel would also have to be considered. The tax rate could be perhaps half as high as that for petroleum. In this way, the competitive status of solar, water, wind and muscle power would further increase and excessive use of bio-fuels be prevented.

To conclude, let us summarise the astonishing conclusions from this chapter. Assuming that market forces are allowed to work, an annual increase in fuel prices of only 5% in real terms seems likely to bring about over two or three decades an absolutely revolutionary transformation of the entire transport system. This conclusion may no longer be seen as quite so astonishing if we remember what an eightfold increase in the cost (for the employer) of human labour has brought about. This change, of course, took a little longer and was not a *planned* increase of a particular price signal. But the transformation resulting (in part) from steadily rising labour costs was no less dramatic than what we have envisioned as a result of fuel price increases in this chapter. After all, in quite literal terms, it has meant a transition from manufacture by hand to the latest developments in robotics. We can expect technological and other changes as a result of sustained increases in fuel prices over several decades of no less a significance and scale. All the more so if our ecological tax reform proposals were extended from energy — the example we have chosen to concentrate on by way of illustrating our general argument — to a range of other natural resource 'inputs' as well.

# 8. Objections and Obstacles to Ecological Tax Reform

In spite of the evident advantages of an ecological tax reform, there are a number of reservations and objections that must be expected or taken note of. The most important objections raised in the public debate over green taxes and the resistance that can be expected are briefly sketched below.

## The Fiscal Policy Objection:
## The conflicting goals of yield vs. steering effect

The German debate over ecological taxes was greatly influenced by a weighty appraisal for the Federal Environment Ministry on the different economic instruments available for environmental policy.[23] The authors, both eminent economists, were professors Dr. Karl-Heinrich Hansmeyer, who served for many years as a member and Chairman of the Council of Experts on environmental questions, and Dr. Hans Karl Schneider, a leading energy expert who also was the academic mentor of the Minister, Prof. Dr. Klaus Töpfer. In the appraisal, the debate over ecological taxes, which flared up anew in 1988, was taken up and criticised in the sharpest terms. The central argument was that ecological taxes, if they are effective, will in the end destroy the very basis of their revenue yield. Taxes, by definition, should have a yield. Hence green taxes are either unacceptable to the finance minister or to the environment minister and should therefore be rejected categorically.

This prognosis of the conflict in goals between yield and steering effectiveness has, since the appearance of the Hansmeyer-

57

Schneider appraisal, formed the central argument both of the German federal government and of the sundry opponents of ecological taxes. Both spokesmen for energy intensive industry and proponents of traditional social policy, with their respective fears of negative distribution effects, found it very convenient to use the innocent-sounding conflicting goals argument to explain why one should, of course, reject this awful new instrument of policy.

There are two principal ways of answering the fiscal policy objection.

(1) A tax rate regime can be established which automatically increases ecological taxes at a specific rate or percentage each year for a certain period of time. Other taxes would be reduced by the full amount raised in ecological taxes. In this way, revenues from ecological taxes grow sufficiently to please the exchequer. At the same time, the steering effect would also grow steadily, which ought to please the environment minister. Obviously this mechanism does not remove the conflict in goals *per se,* but the conflict is no longer a reasonable ground for categorically rejecting the instrument of an ecological tax reform.

When after a certain time the steering effect becomes so strong that revenues are really shrinking (as was speculated in the context of Fig. 15), then the State will have to resort to more conventional taxes again (or to new ecological taxes).

(2) A similar means of overcoming the problem of conflicting goals might be to establish a certain tax revenue target and to adjust tax rates accordingly every year. This procedure likewise satisfies the exchequer's needs. But it has the disadvantage of making prices of the taxed commodities, notably energy and material prices, unpredictable.

There is a historical example of an ecological tax in which a fixed revenue target was defined: the Japanese $SO_2$ tax. Revenue from the tax had to be maintained at an essentially constant level since it was earmarked for a fund designed to compensate pollution victims (so it was actually a special charge, not a tax). Advances in the technical control of emissions then led to an unexpectedly rapid decline in $SO_2$ emissions. Consequently, the tax rate had to be drastically increased and soon reached a level five hundred times higher than in the beginning! To be sure, the Japanese economy as a whole was never substantially damaged by this. Although there was a strong rise in electricity prices, the production of flue gas desulphurisation systems was given a major boost, and the economy quickly learned to live with higher power costs.

The scenarios set out in Chapter 7 clearly follow the first of the two above-mentioned ways in that they propose an annual increase in constant dollars of 5-7% in the cost of relevant factors.

## The Social Policy Objection: 'Green taxes aren't fair'

Ecological taxes, and particularly taxes on energy, have a tendency to hit the less well-off layers of society relatively harder than the more affluent ones.[24] This is a characteristic of almost all indirect taxes, especially of value added tax. The reason for this is that these taxes raise the prices of the basic things of life, which make up a smaller percentage in the shopping basket of the more well to do. While energy costs in wealthy households come to between 2.5% and 3.5% of annual expenditure, with pensioners, the unemployed and other less well-off people, it is often in the region of or above 5%. Fig. 16 shows the social distribution impact of ecological taxation.

Hansmeyer and Schneider (see note 21) and German industry (e.g. H. Förster[25] cheerfully make use of the social policy objection as a sort of respectable support for their general rejection of ecological taxes. But there are also numerous warning voices from traditional left-wing parties.

To answer this objection it may be useful to do some arithmetic. Let us assume that energy taxes are raised at a rate of

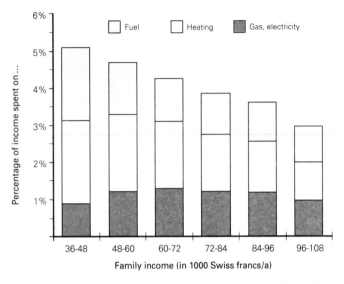

**Fig 16:** Energy costs as a percentage of annual expenditure for Swiss households with various incomes (in Swiss francs). Source: Mauch, et al. (note 22)

5% per annum. Let us also assume that energy productivity, or macroeconomic energy efficiency according to the term used in Chapter 6, is increasing at a rate of 3% per annum (which is a modest estimate). Then the average additional expenditure on energy (assuming no increase in use) would be 2% per annum. If energy costs make up 5% of expenses in less well-off households, then the *added* annual costs resulting from energy taxes would be only 0.1% on average which is not a figure to worry about in any major way.

If there was, furthermore, a political consensus to reduce VAT *pari passu* with increased energy taxes, then all potentially remaining negative distributional effects would disappear because the distribution effects of VAT are very similar to that of an energy tax.

Moreover, expanding public transport and simultaneously increasing the cost of air travel and heavy automobiles would actually have a positive distribution effect. (This is even more valid, by the way, for developing countries in which owning a car is still very much an exceptional privilege. Also domestic use of commercial energy is still correlated with affluence in the developing countries.)

Nevertheless, for reasons of political psychology (rather than out of a real concern for equity) it may be useful to offer the ecological tax reform proposal in a package which includes some social measures to compensate the poorer strata of society for at least part of the added energy bill.

Finally, it must be said with regard to the social policy objection that the destruction of the environment is in itself regressive in that it hits the poor harder than the affluent, who are far better able to escape its impact. If ecological tax reform is viewed as being an indispensable element in the ecological healing process, then it will be promoted precisely for reasons of social policy.

## The Environmental Policy Objection: 'Revenue should be purpose-linked'

Environmental policy makers and the environmental interest groups tend to be preoccupied with the need for public expenditure for the sake of the environment. Comparing the budget of the environment minister with that of the social welfare or defence minister, one is tempted to believe that the environment minister's influence is far too small. Given this background, it is also tempting to believe that clearly all revenues from ecologically motivated taxes should flow directly into the coffers of the environment ministry and should be earmarked for urgent environmental tasks. Public acceptance, too, tends to be higher for purpose-linked charges than for taxes simply filling the coffers of a greedy, anonymous state. In terms of the words we use, that would prompt us to call them not ecological taxes, but special charges. Practically all of the charge instruments found by Hans Opschoor (see note 12) in the 14

OECD countries he studied were called administrative charges, user charges or effluent charges.

Naturally, it would be desirable both for the environment and for the environment minister if the proceeds from ecological taxes were placed directly at his or her disposal. But, as has been argued in Chapter 3, only an ecological tax reform has a chance to reach the magnitude of 5-10% of GNP, while earmarked charges are restricted for economic reasons to very much smaller amounts. As indicated in Fig. 3, a large scale tax reform leads to much better environmental results than a small special charge.

Moreover, the legislature is always free to decide on spending priorities for non-earmarked revenues. Assuming, for instance, that the price increase of petrol leads to more demand for railway freight and passenger services, then one should expect broad parliamentary consensus on spending for public transport at the expense of the highway construction budget. For the environment it would not matter too much whether it was the environment minister or the transport minister who was spending the money to improve rail services.

Similarly, it is possible to conceive of a parliamentary decision to establish a fund for the protection of tropical forests, or for an urgent clean-up programme, even if there was no formal earmarking of the revenues from an ecological tax beforehand.

## The Economic Policy Objection:
## 'Ecological taxes are a burden on the economy'

If ecological taxes are viewed merely as a means of increasing the cost of environmentally relevant production factors, one would fear that such taxes would damage the competitiveness of the economy. If, however, revenue neutrality is strictly observed, the damage would be counterbalanced by equivalent additional competitive advantages for those sectors that pay less taxes *because* of the reform.

Even so, some authors including Bergmann and Ewringmann[26] argue that even a revenue-neutral ecological tax reform places a burden on the economy, in that it leads to avoidance investments that would normally not have been made. If the money devoted to such efforts is reducing funds otherwise available for investments in expansion and innovation, the reform might indeed work as a deadweight on the economy and competitiveness problems could theoretically ensue. But, in fairness, one should also ask how much money today is already being spent on 'avoidance' investments against excessive labour costs, and how much of that is made profitable only due to the high taxes on human labour and how much society then has to pay for additional unemployment.

A careful, critical analysis should be made to find out whether or not an ecological tax reform works as a burden on the economy and how the burden — if any — can be avoided by appropriately adjusting the taxes. Such analysis cannot be done in a few pages. It will have to take into account local and international circumstances and specific and theoretical considerations. In any case, there are strong reasons to believe that a gradual change in business conditions stimulating higher efficiency in the use of scarce natural resources should work as a relief, not as a burden, for the economy as a whole.

A slowly progressing, revenue-neutral ecological tax reform with provisions to prevent the ruin of any large scale sector of the economy should be a relatively safe bet. And to make the comparison fair, it should be assessed against other measures that might otherwise be resorted to in order to slow down and ultimately reverse the dynamics of greenhouse gas emissions and to combat other global ecological disasters. Much will depend on the appropriateness of the price signal. The process of change should move forward at a pace which does not overtax an economy's innovative strength and readiness to invest. Furthermore, the greatest possible degree of international harmonisation should be sought, as we will argue later in this chapter.

One more concern has to be considered — *inflation*. Green taxes have an inbuilt tendency to spur inflation because they increase specifically the prices of goods which feature prominently in the basket of goods and services from which inflation rates are calculated. The easiest answer to this concern is compensatory reductions in other indirect taxes, notably VAT, which have a very similar influence on inflation. But in the end a truly revenue-neutral tax reform should not have a major effect on inflation. Initial inflationary effects should, in theory, be compensated for over time by tax reductions in other parts of the economy. It can even be argued that increased resource efficiency may ultimately have anti-inflationary effects.

These positive effects could come from two different corners: (1) if gross labour costs are reduced, positive employment effects could ensue which would relieve public budgets of an unemployment welfare payments burden and spur the economy further; (2) if the ecological tax reform creates a new and more reliable sense of direction for investments, the climate for investments may improve and the overall balance of spending may be shifted from consumption to investment. Further reasons for expecting beneficial economic effects from an ecological tax reform are presented in Chapter 10.

What should not be denied is the fact that there are going to be losers. Among these will be the following sectors — mining (abroad as well as at home), power plant construction, truck manufacturers, bulk chemicals, cement, and metal smelting plants (especially aluminium smelting from bauxite). Some sectors will find it impossible to hold out in their present form, and would have to emigrate. Aluminium companies would have to boost the recycling rate and expand their business with the aluminium service sector (which helps to save energy in other ways), and would in general have to diversify. But there is no pressing ecological reason why the losers should not be permitted to allow their existing plant to completely depreciate. At the same time, however, there is also no *economic* reason to keep on investing in ecologically unsustainable ways of production.

## The Voter Objection: 'Ecological taxes aren't popular'

Any politician worried about votes will necessarily be reluctant to introduce new taxes. In recent elections in several countries including the USA and Germany, conservative governments, by absolutely pledging neither to increase taxes nor to introduce new ones, won resounding victories over opponents who either for ecological reasons or out of honesty, declared it was unavoidable to raise taxes and/or introduce ecological taxes. Given this background, it would appear that introducing ecological taxes without reducing other taxes to the greatest possible extent would be politically very difficult. However, polls have confirmed time and again that a clear majority are in favour of the introduction of ecological taxes if they do not increase the overall fiscal burden.

The most important political task confronting those advocating an ecological tax reform is public information. It must be very clearly stated that ecological tax reform is not being introduced to finance environmental pipedreams. On the other hand, where there are already devastating budget deficits such as in the United States, Italy and Germany, it would not be wrong to use a portion of the revenue that results from green taxes for the purpose of reducing the deficit for a limited period. In this way — highly desirable both from a social and ecological standpoint — the trend towards higher interest rates could be weakened or reversed.

The hypothesis that an ecological tax reform would increase rather than decrease the amount of wealth available for distribution must be demonstrated in the most concrete and credible terms possible. Also, the failure of existing pollution control policies to address the global environmental problems effectively should be openly admitted, thus creating a desire on the part of the general public to do better. And the term 'ecological tax' should consistently be replaced by 'ecological tax *reform.*'

Above all, a cross-party consensus on ecological tax reform must be brought into being well in advance of any forthcoming important elections, thus preventing the reform from becoming a source of political dispute between the parties during the campaign. It should be clear to all responsible political parties that any idea of a significant, albeit slow, pace for introducing an ecological tax reform must hinge on a broad political consensus which must not be put in question at every election. The consensus should reach the kind of stability enjoyed today by, for example, the necessity for a good educational system or social security.

## The Effectiveness Objection:
## 'There are instruments which work faster and with greater precision than ecological taxes.'

Particularly in environmentalist circles, simply increasing the cost of environmentally harmful behaviour through taxation is often viewed as immoral: 'The rich can buy their way out; it'll just be the poor who are forced to behave ecologically.' For impatient environmentalists, clear-cut bans, ambitious standards, strict liability regulations, and strict environmental impact assessments in any planning process are considerably more appealing. In these circles, the ways in which costs ensuing from ecological taxes are passed on in higher prices is considered to be immoral, too, and are frequently cited as an argument against the effectiveness of ecological taxes.

Naturally, there are environmental challenges and tasks for which ecological taxes are not the answer. The ban on DDT and the impending prohibition of CFCs are certainly to be preferred over a mere tax-induced increase in the cost of the relevant substances (although in the case of those CFCs which are extremely useful substances for certain purposes, a charge-refund system might actually work faster and more efficiently than a ban which is not easily accepted by and enforced in countries like India or China). When there is immediate danger or when there is an acute health hazard, quick and drastic measures are needed. Nature conservancy and the protection of biodiversity, as well as the licensing of potentially hazardous industrial facilities, require conventional command and control measures including tougher liability laws, appropriate environmental impact studies, free access to environmental information plus some of the more conventional economic instruments.

However, the scenarios set out in Chapter 7 show to an impressive degree how a consistent ecological tax reform will result in a degree of steering influence that would be virtually inconceivable using conventional environmental policy instruments. In this way, an ecological tax reform would be clearly above moral reproach. The changes, after all, would affect rich and poor to an equal degree and would in the end provide the less well-off elements of society with decent public transport, something for which people have been waiting in vain in the vast majority of countries.

Economists like Holger Bonus[27] assert that economic instruments are likely to be twice as efficient as comparable regulatory measures. This is particularly relevant in view of the regulatory camp's hopes that fuel efficiency in automobiles and heating efficiency in buildings can be brought about through obligatory efficiency standards. The result of this is sure to be far removed from the optimum path of transformation we have argued is necessary and possible, given an ecological tax reform.

Once again, it should be emphasised that the enormous effectiveness one can expect from an ecological tax reform has much to do with the long-term reliability, and hence predicability, of the process.

## The Inertia Objection:
## 'Ecological taxes will throw everything into disorder'

In wealthy countries, a fiscal system based primarily on income taxes and value added taxes has made itself quite at home. Environmental problems, it is thought, have been brought at least somewhat under control by regulatory means, complemented to an extent by special charges, liability law, public spending on the environment and some environmental education. Given this perception, plunging the fiscal system — with its complicated distribution of revenue at local, state and federal, in the European case, EC levels and its intricate system of deductions — together with the current array of environmental instruments, into complete uncertainty by introducing ecological taxes is a somewhat implausible course of action for tough-minded *realpolitiker*. From the standpoint of *realpolitik,* the inertia objection could be the most weighty of all. Without a broad sense that there is an ecological crisis, it is likely to be very difficult indeed to introduce an entirely innovative instrument.

Switzerland or the Scandinavian countries may possibly prove less sluggish and hostile to innovation than the larger EC countries. They could (and probably will) serve as pioneer countries. But even in the EC, at least at the Commission level, and at all of the large environmental associations within the EC, the view that ecological taxes are desirable is now gaining the upper hand. The EC Commission came up with an important proposal in September 1991 [28], as we shall see in the next section.

In any case, a gradually introduced ecological tax reform will certainly be able to cope with the inertia objection better than any abruptly introduced reform that might eventually become suddenly necessary if the world delays taking effective action at this stage.


## The Harmonisation Objection:
## 'Ecological taxes cannot be harmonised within the EC'

If one assumes that every environmental policy measure is a burden on the economy and will necessarily cause competi-tiveness problems at home, one would immediately wonder whether environmental laws are truly susceptible to being internationally harmonised. If the measures hold out a promise of working in an economically advantageous manner, however, the process of harmonisation should be much easier. This is an argument for ecological taxes as an instrument of EC environmental policy, or in the case of the USA, at federal level. A smaller harmonisation problem may arise in relation to specific taxes. Article 99 of the EEC Treaty, for example, asks for harmonisation of indirect taxes, thereby theoretically excluding the introduction at national level of green taxes before an EC-wide regime is established. But in practice there is scope for at least a certain individuality on the part of member countries, as has been allowed in the case of VAT.

Moreover, it was the Commission itself which took the first major initiative within the Community for introducing ecological taxes. In their proposal[28] the Commission suggests, among a few other measures in the context of the fight against the accelerating greenhouse effect, the introduction in seven steps of fossil fuel taxes up to the level of $10 per barrel oil equivalent and half that fiscal burden for nuclear energy. The Commission also proposes strict budget neutrality and would allow some energy-intensive sectors to receive time-limited tax exemptions.

It may be worth mentioning in the EC context that an ecological tax reform should be highly attractive to those very countries whose poverty would normally be an obstacle to harmonisation. This is because an environmental policy with relatively little in the way of administrative expenses and with the prospect of economic gain would, for such countries — Portugal or Greece spring to mind — presumably be more attractive than the present policy of imposing maximum permissible levels of pollution.

* * *

Along with all these objections that have been analysed above — and which should be taken seriously — there are a host of nine-day wonder objections which are essentially the result of misunderstandings. For instance, the occasional claim that ecological taxes are a form of 'strangle taxation' and are unconstitutional to boot, or the fear that ecological taxes are meant to *replace* existing regulatory measures, thus allowing any polluter who promptly pays his taxes to go on spewing filth into the environment. Or the fear that the tax bureaucracy could balloon enormously — which is a failure to recognise the fact that an ecological tax can and should be conceived of as simplifying and facilitating both the tax system and environmental policy.

## Objections from the Losers

Along with political and scientific objections, outright resistance must of course also be reckoned with. This will come primarily from those who feel that they will be materially worse off as a result of ecological taxes. Broadly speaking, these include all those who consume natural resources to an above average extent, or otherwise place an over-proportional burden on, or even destroy, nature. The relevant branches of the economy were indicated earlier in this chapter.

Losers can also mean specific population groups. First and foremost, motorists, but also frequent flyers, owners of detached homes, luxury hotel guests, big meat-eaters, and many others.

The organised representatives of labour, the retired and the unemployed could also offer political resistance if they lacked trust in the intended social neutrality of ecological tax reform, or sensed the chance of a redistribution in their favour if their negotiating stance were sufficiently tough.

Without a broad mobilisation of winners and environmentalists, and without socially and economically acceptable arrangements, a broad and durable political consensus on ecological tax reform cannot be expected.

# 9. The International Dimension

## Industrialised Countries

The industrialised countries are far and away the largest per capita consumers of natural resources. It is in these countries that the introduction of an effective instrument for reducing the consumption of natural resources is most necessary. Furthermore, it is here where political majorities may be most readily found for stringent environmental policies and where there is already a widespread perception that such measures can be afforded. If a step-by-step, revenue-neutral, socially acceptable ecological tax reform promises even to bring economic advantages rather than disadvantages, then no industrialised country should be expected to categorically reject it in the long run.

Indeed, numerous political initiatives are now under way in Europe for introducing ecological taxes. Sweden has introduced a package. Norway, Finland and the Netherlands have introduced elements of ecological taxes into petrol or other taxes. Switzerland and Austria are having lively debates about proposals, and the idea is gaining ground.[29] Most importantly, as was said in Chapter 8, the EC Commission has come up with a proposal for a gradually increasing energy tax, although this does not extend to taxing other natural resources, as we propose.

In the former socialist countries of the North, it has been recognised that their artificially low energy and raw material prices were an essential reason for economic mismanagement. One of the first steps demanded (also by international monetary institutions) has been the raising of petrol, electricity and water prices. A continuation of this trend, vital if these economies are to be returned to good health, would appear to be advisable. To be sure, the economy and societies of Eastern Europe and the former Soviet Union first have to digest their initial price shock. Future conceivable reduction obligations (e.g. of $CO_2$) which, within the context of international environmental accords, could soon be affecting Eastern Europe, ought to be able to be introduced almost automatically during the course of the economic reforms now being set into motion. Thus, from the Western point of view, it is entirely conceivable that, at the start of an ecological tax reform, explicit harmonisation with the East would be unnecessary.

Great difficulties, however, can be expected from the United States, whose cultural and economic make-up is linked to unlimited mobility and whose economic philosophy only grudgingly allows for the use of fiscal influences on energy prices. But progress in Western Europe and Japan does not depend on American acquiescence. On the whole, the already relatively high energy prices in Western Europe and Japan have not brought about any competitive disadvantages for these countries *vis-à-vis* the United States. On the contrary, during the last 15 years those economies that have maintained high energy price levels at home have developed particularly well. This astonishing fact is indicated in Fig. 17.

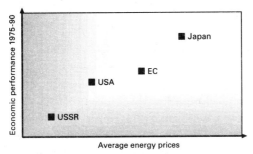

**Fig. 17:** The economic performance of the four largest economic blocks does not seem to have suffered as a result of high energy prices; quite the contrary. Economic success can be defined as a somewhat arbitrary mix of growth in GNP per capita, the external trade balance, the stock market index, and full employment (for which data for the former Soviet Union either do not exist, or exist only in a loose sense).

One can, of course, quickly object that the figure merely reflects the differing economic structures of the four blocs. On the other hand, it is precisely these structures which are closely linked to energy prices. Japanese industry's switch to knowledge-intensive products was greatly accelerated by high energy prices, while the antiquated heavy industry of the Soviet Union was preserved — on purpose or inadvertently — by subsidised energy prices.

## Developing Countries

Today, many developing countries appear on the world market primarily as suppliers of natural resources and as debtors. The two characteristics are bound together in a tragic manner. Debt servicing has forced raw material exporters to throw more and more primary materials on to the market, thus leading to a general fall in prices and to yet more feverish sales of raw materials. Fig. 18 shows the connection.

An artificial dampening of demand for raw materials and energy on the part of the North — by means of an ecological tax reform — could have the serious effect of further aggravating the problem for many countries of the South.

In the following section, an examination of the impact of ecological taxes on developing countries will be made. Attention will be focused on four possible situations:

(1) An ecological tax reform is introduced in the industrialised countries only. What impact will this have on:
- a) raw material importers?
- b) raw material exporters?

(2) An ecological tax reform is introduced in both industrialised and developing countries. What impact will this have on:
- a) raw material importers?
- b) raw material exporters?

1979-81=100                                          Billion US$

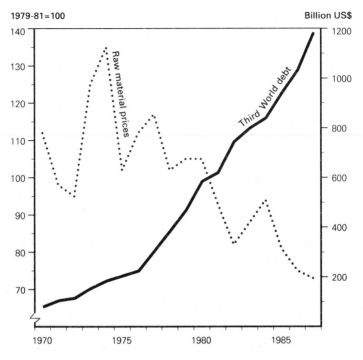

**Fig. 18:** Development of raw material prices and Third World debt from 1970 to 1989. (From Lester Brown et al., *State of the World 1990* (note 1) p.144.

## (1) The impact of an ecological tax reform in the industrialised countries on the developing world

### a) Effects on raw material importers

The successful implementation of an ecological tax reform in the rich countries of the North will lead, as has been shown by our elasticity analysis, to a drastic mid- and long-term fall in demand for taxed inputs (notably oil and other raw materials). As a result, if the fall in demand is felt worldwide, further decreases in world market prices for these products would have to be expected.

For those developing countries who themselves are net importers of raw materials (and, so far as energy is concerned, they constitute the majority of developing countries), this could lead to an overall improvement in the balance of payments. For funds which, up until then, had to be spent on importing oil could now be used for satisfying other requirements, for instance the import of capital goods. Remember that the high import prices for oil in the mid-1970s wrought great destruction on the already fragile economies of the non-oil countries of the South — which soon led to the coining of the new term Fourth World or Least Developed Countries (LLDC). Their economic difficulties would probably, at least in this respect, be lessened as a result of a policy of voluntary limits on energy consumption in the industrialised countries.

Along with this, it should be pointed out that the technologies of resource efficiency and solar energy exploitation are significantly better suited to these countries than the kind of technology which predominates today. If many industrialised countries were allocating major financial and technical resources for the development of high efficiency technologies (e.g. the mass production of cars with extremely low petrol consumption), the spreading into the Third World of these new technologies could be expected with little time lag. Viewed in this way, these countries of the Third World which are net importers of energy and raw materials stand to profit from the introduction of an ecological tax reform in the North at least to some degree.

### b) Effects on raw material exporters

The situation is quite different for those who are primarily raw material exporters — whether they be oil and gas exporters, or exporters of other raw materials falling within the ambit of an ecological tax reform. An ecological tax reform in the North and the associated fall in demand would mean that these countries would stand to lose a substantial, not to say overwhelming, part of their export earnings. It is only a partial consolation that this development would be fairly slow and might well be accompanied by more or less compensating demand increases on the part of the newly industrialising countries and some other developing countries

The principal hope for Third World countries, however, would have to lie in the fact that the purchasing power of the industrialised countries would not shrink and would gradually be redirected to more refined products, thus offering the South an improved chance for non-commodity exports. Obviously, it would be essential that the North remove the significant trade barriers that remain against manufactured products from the South.

It should also be emphasised that mining and selling one's natural resources are not in the long run a sustainable path of development by definition. For raw material exporting countries, the most important renewable resource is their manpower. This is in many cases very poorly developed and focused all too frequently on the exploitation of non-renewable resources. The obvious and economically sensible thing to do would be to invest much of today's export earnings into tomorrow's business opportunities. Such long-term strategies should be encouraged, not discouraged, by the North. The gains, in terms of an improved balance of payments that the rich countries of the North will make as a result of ecological tax reform, ought at least in part to be reinvested in the affected raw material exporting countries, and in ways that promote sustainable development.

It is very much in the interest of the North that political stability be maintained in the oil and other natural resource exporting countries of the South. For this reason, also, a gradual process of ecological tax reform that allows raw material exporters time to adjust would be advisable.

## (2) Ecological tax reform in the developing countries

### a) Effects on raw material importers
Leaving aside all environmental considerations, taxes on imported raw materials have the same effect as import duties. They raise the price of the imported good, reduce demand and thus improve the balance of payments. On the other hand, import duties tend to provoke trading partners into taking equivalent

measures, and so may reduce the economic gains to be made in foreign trade. They are thus rightly condemned by economists in most circumstances.

However, when it comes to green taxes imposed on account of overriding ecological considerations, such levies on imported raw materials are highly desirable. In this case, the consumption of the goods taxed is *supposed* to go down or to be kept low, not so much for reasons of the balance of payments, but in order to place a damper on the negative ecological effects of these goods.

In reality, however, many developing countries have an awkward tradition, not unlike the former socialist countries, of subsidising the use of water, petrol and electricity, even though (or perhaps because?) only a small rich minority who can afford automobiles, air conditioners, etc. actually benefit from this. Such subsidies — aside from the distribution effects — are also nonsensical from a macro-economic point of view since they artificially boost demand for imported goods which generally have to be paid for using hard currency, while at the same time the abundant factor of production labour, is made more expensive through the taxation that is necessary to finance the subsidies. This sort of situation tends to lead to an increase in unemployment and a lower level of economic efficiency.

In contrast to this, an ecologically motivated fuel tax in the South would simultaneously:

- Reduce car traffic, which has reached an unbearable level in such mega-cities of the developing world as Cairo, Lagos, Sao Paulo and Bangkok;

- Offer the possibility of using the revenue to stabilise public finances and thus limit inflation and reduce the tax burden on labour and corporate activity;

- Improve the composition of imports inasmuch as, for instance, capital goods could be imported instead of petroleum;

- And help to reduce conflicts that invariably arise around the construction of giant dams, conventional or nuclear power plants, large scale tree felling or the opening of big mining complexes.

In short, for raw material importing countries in the South as in the North, an ecological tax reform could prove to be an economic blessing not only from the standpoint of equity and the environment, but also in terms of improved economic performance. Of course, serious problems of political acceptance are likely to surface precisely on account of those effects on distribution which we view so positively. This is because the elite, which would be the part of society primarily affected adversely by these measures, is unlikely to accept passively an increase in their cost of living. Much would depend on getting the message across to the ruling classes of the developing countries that the immediate disadvantages are far outweighed by the medium- and long-term gains resulting from an improvement in their countries' economic structures and the reduction of environmental problems. Furthermore, within the context of international environmental accords, it is conceivable that the North could participate in cushioning the losses incurred as a result.

*b) Effects on raw material exporters*
The situation is somewhat different for those developing countries which themselves dispose over the relevant natural resources. An increase in the cost of these raw materials domestically would improve neither the balance of payments nor the economic structure, since there is of course no shortage of these raw materials. Here, too, however, the ecological arguments for imposing a green tax of the kind we are proposing are valid, particularly when the exploitation of raw materials has a long-term adverse impact on a country. This applies, for instance, to tropical forest resources: in response to a short-term foreign exchange emergency, some countries are quite literally sawing off the branch they're sitting on.

And here also, subsidised fuel, electricity, etc. benefit primarily the wealthier social strata, and at the expense of the poorer elements of society. Even if the OPEC countries are hardly likely to see the need to tax their lavishly flowing oil, an effort could at least be made towards dismantling subsidies of this sort.

Raw material exporting developing countries such as most of OPEC (but also China) will be the hardest to convince that they should do their part in saving natural resources and reducing global ecological problems by taxing and thereby increasing the cost of the raw materials at their disposal. Only once the industrialised countries have moved forward and demonstrated that they are making economic gains, is it likely that the raw material exporting developing countries will come around to a policy of ecological renewal.

# 10. What Makes Ecological Tax Reform Attractive for the Business World?

Hardly any major political change is realistically conceivable these days that is not explicitly welcomed or at least tolerated by the private sector. Therefore it is important to assess the likely reactions of the business community to the idea of an ecological tax reform, and in terms more explicit than the general answers given in Chapter 8 to the economic policy objection.

Ecological tax reform should significantly improve resource efficiency both on the micro- and macro-economic levels. Any investment that leads to output being maintained but with a substantially smaller input of resources (provided such gains in efficiency only require a reasonable level of investment expenditure) must be seen cumulatively leading to a macro-economic advantage. Disposable wealth as a result is bound to increase rather than decrease in the wake of an ecological tax reform. A steering effect which brings about an enhanced quality of life and a reduction in external costs in, for instance, the areas of medical care or pollution control ought to increase the amount of *net* wealth that can be distributed, even if there were no additional growth in *gross* national product.

For the business world, a long-term strategy of a revenue-neutral and gradual ecological tax reform could become a highly attractive political goal. Clearly, the business world — like anyone else — is not going to favour an abandonment of other, more familiar policy elements. But there are a number of reasons why business could come out in favour of such a long-term tax reform strategy. Reviewing these reasons is an appropriate way of bringing this short book to a conclusion.

(1) For business, long-term predictability is of first-rate importance. Were one to compare the concept of a quantitatively predictable tax reform running over a period of two to four decades with the leaps and bounds of current environmental policy and the incalculability and unpredictability of, say, the market for crude oil (on which the modern industrial economy will necessarily become increasingly dependent, the longer resource saving strategies are put off), an ecological tax reform ought to result in significant gains due to its enabling the private sector to avoid numerous false investment trails as well as due to its creation of an environment conducive to a stable and continuous process of innovation.

(2) For the economy — just as much as for the Earth's population — an effective strategy for reducing or even solving the global environmental problems that threaten (see Chapter 1) is something which is highly desirable. A positive commitment on the part of industry to such a strategy (rather than a merely grudging toleration of it) would, moreover, contribute positively to the building of a new image of industry and to the emergence of a new fundamental consensus in our societies. For its part, the formation of a consensus will have a further stabilising effect and so make possible more reliable predictions and again contribute to the safety of investments. A greatly to be desired consensus on energy policy would at last be within reach.

(3) If increased efficiency overall in the handling of scarce resources represents an economic gain, industry will also benefit from it. Likewise, it would by no means be the last to benefit from the economic gains which could result from a reduction in existing taxes on business profits, value added and gainful employment. And if private households begin to make energy-, water- and material-saving investments for their homes, in preference to forms of short-lived consumption like on frequent long distance travel, it could lead to an increase in demand for many industrial products. A whole new industrial growth sector might emerge.

Industry also plays a role as a customer of the capital goods sector and of consultancy and will increase its demand for innovative goods and services.

(4) The fact that an ecological tax reform can be put into force in developing countries in practice (and not merely on paper) and can perhaps be made politically acceptable in such countries, elevates this instrument well above the bureaucracy-intensive regulatory instruments as regards the potential for *international harmonisation*. Certainly harmonisation of pollution control standards between countries of different levels of development has so far proven exceedingly difficult.

This would make it easier for international companies to extend their philosophy of identical standards worldwide (which at present only applies to certain limited pollution control commitments) to the whole area of resource efficiency. Companies will have to watch out for criticism of their international operations with regard to the high rate of natural resource consumption (*and* pollution) involved in the early stages of production. These early stages of production typically are located in poor countries with often non-existent environmental controls.

(5) As soon as an ecological tax reform of the kind we propose shows visible signs of ecological success, it would become defensible to clear out the current regulatory thicket and significantly reduce the environmental bureaucracy presiding over it. On the other hand, if present rates of environmental destruction continue, public pressure could escalate sharply in favour of a further tightening of command and control instruments, including much more far-reaching liability laws which could turn almost every investment into an incalculable risk.

(6) A shifting of technological development in the direction of high sophistication/low waste production again makes this instrument distinctly innovation-friendly. Countries and regions

following this strategy are bound to obtain a competitive edge in modern production over those persisting with conventional methods of production and mere bureaucratic innovation policies. This should also make for a highly attractive business climate for the high sophistication sectors of production.

(7) Finally, failure to adapt to the global environmental crisis at an early stage could become exceedingly expensive later on. But if we begin early, we still seem to have time for that slow, profitable, no ruptures strategy.

\* \* \*

Obviously, these reasons will appeal to different companies and industries to a very varying degree. And each one depends on an ecological tax reform being instituted slowly, reliably, on a long-term basis, and as an integral part of a credible policy mix.

The best guarantee of an *economically* sustainable reform process would be an initiative from the business community to join hands with sensible environmentalists and politicians in designing an effective and reliable strategy of sustainable development in North and South.

The Business Council for Sustainable Development appears to have taken such an initiative. In its final report, *Changing Course*,[30] a strong emphasis can be seen on prices reflecting ecological realities. This could well become the starting point for a joint strategy between business leaders and environmentalists.

# Notes and References

1.  World Commission on Environment and Development, *Our Common Future,* (often referred to as the Brundtland Report) Oxford University Press, 1987. Other books give plenty of factual information on the state of the global environment including policy options. There is the annual *State of the World,* produced by the Worldwatch Institute, Washington D.C., edited by Lester Brown et al., and published by W.W. Norton, New York. Also very recommendable is *World Resources,* edited jointly by the World Resources Institute, Washington D.C. and UNDP and UNEP, Oxford University Press, 1990. One of the authors of *Ecological Tax Reform* is preparing an updated English edition of a comprehensive analysis (in German) of ecological world affairs and policy options: Ernst U. von Weizsäcker, *Erdpolitik — Ökologische Realpolitik an der Schwelle zum Jahrhundert der Umwelt,* Wissenschaftliche Buchgesellschaft, Darmstadt, 1990. This updated English edition to be published as *Earth Politics After the Earth Summit,* Zed Books: London, Autumn 1992.
2.  This unconventional graph was first used and published by IG Metall, *Auto, Umwelt und Verkehr,* Volume 122, Verlag IG Metall, Frankfurt a. M. 1990, p. 42.
3.  Intergovernmental Panel on Climate Change, The IPCC Scientific Assessment, edited by J.T. Houghton, G.J. Jenkins, J.J. Ephraums, Cambridge: Cambridge University Press, 1990.
    Intergovernmental Panel on Climate Change, The IPCC Impacts Assessment, edited by J. McG Tegart, G.W.Sheldon, D. C. Griffiths, Canberra: Australian Government Publishing Service, 1990.
    Intergovernmental Panel on Climate Change, The IPCC Responses Strategies, World Meteorological Organisation/United Nations Environment Programme 1990, available as a manuscript from WMO, Geneva.
4.  Illustration based on the work of the German Bundestag's Committee of Enquiry (English translation:) 'Protection of the Earth's Atmosphere', *Protecting the Earth: A Status Report with Recommendations for a New Energy Policy,* Bundestag, Bonn, 1991.
5.  See for example: Catherine Caufield, *Multiple Exposures: Chronicles of the Radiation Age.* Penguin Books, London, 1989.
6.  See for example Daniel Deudney, Christopher Flavin, *Renewable Energy: The Power to Choose,* W.W. Norton: New York and London, 1983; or P.O'Keefe and N.N. Pearsall (eds), *Renewable Energy Sources for the 21st Century,* Adam Hilger, 1988.

7. Dennis A. Meadows et al., *Limits to Growth*, Report to the Club of Rome, Universe Books, New York, 1972.

8. Ernst U. von Weizsäcker, 'Sustainability — A Task for the North', *Journal of International Affairs*, Vol. 44, No. 2, Winter 1991, pp 421-32.

9. Cf. Bundestag Committee of Enquiry (previously cited — note 4) p. 68. Eberhard Jochem estimates the long-term technical potential for energy saving at 80-90% in: *Stellungnahme im Rahmen einer Anhörung Enquetekommission 'Vorsorge zum Schutz der Erdatmosphäre'* of the 11th German Federal Parliament dated June 20, 1988, Kommissionsdrucksache 11/32, p. 70. In its Third Volume (quoted in note 4), the Committee of Enquiry used a figure of at least 50% for the theoretical potential of reducing energy consumption without reducing energy service quality. Both figures do not take into account possible *systemic* substitutions (e.g. vegetables for meat, or rail for road).

10. e.g. Johannes B. Opschoor and Hans Vos, *The Application of Economic Instruments for Environmental Protection in OECD Member Countries*, OECD: Paris, 1989; or David Pearce et al., *Blueprint for A Green Economy*, Earthscan Publications, London, 1989. An excellent if less scientific overview is provided by Frances Cairncross, *Costing the Earth: What Governments Must Do; What Consumers Need to Know; How Business Can Profit*, The Economist Books: London, 1991.

11. Cf. D. Pearce et al., op.cit., p. 31. The classic work is: W.H. Dales, *Pollution, Property and Prices*, Toronto, 1968.

12. Michael J. Grubb, *The Greenhouse Effect — Negotiating Targets*, Royal Institute of International Affairs: London, 1989.

13. Frances Cairncross, op.cit., p. 96 -9.

14. The graph is from Ernst U. von Weizsäcker, *Erdpolitik*, op. cit., p. 160.

15. Lutz Wicke, *Die ökologischen Milliarden: Das kostet die zerstörte Umwelt — so können wir sie retten*, Kösel: Munich, 1986. Cf. also Frances Cairncross, op.cit., pp. 23-34; and Per-Olov Johanson, 'Valuing Environmental Damage', *Oxford Review of Economic Policy*, Vol. 6, 1990, p. 46ff.

16. The graph is from Ernst U. von Weizsäcker, *Erdpolitik*, op.cit., p. 147.

17. Arthur Cecil Pigou, *The Economics of Welfare*, London: Macmillan,1920. This British tradition has been taken up by, among others Professor Malcolm Slesser at the University of Edinburgh and by Farel Bradbury (in his *The Delight of Resource Economics*, Ross-on-Wye, 1989).

18. Cf. for instance, T. Sterner, *The Pricing of and Demand for Gasoline*, Swedish Transport Research Board: Stockholm, 1990. Sterner sets a *short-term* average price elasticity in OECD countries of 0.24 and a *long-term* price elasticity of 0.79 !

19. For those readers who would like to know more about the methodology employed in these price elasticity calculations, the relevant author, Jochen

Jesinghaus, can be contacted c/o Wuppertal Institute for Climate, Environment and Energy, P.O.Box 10 04 80, D-5600 Wuppertal 1 (Germany).

20. Further information available from Jochen Jesinghaus (see previous footnote).
21. George Heaton et al., *Transforming Technology: An Agenda for Environmentally Sustainable Growth in the 21st Century*, World Resources Institute; Washington D.C., April 1990, p. 12ff.
22. Cf. for instance, 'Brennstoffzelle macht E-PKW zum agilen Langstreckler'. by Helmut Schiller in *VDI-Nachrichten*, July 5, 1991, p. 18.
23. Karl-Heinrich Hansmeyer and Hans Karl Schneider, *Fortentwicklung der Umweltpolitik unter marktsteuernden Aspekten*, Federal Environment Ministry: Bonn, 1989.
24. Samuel Mauch and Rolf Iten, *Ökologische Steuerreform — Fallbeispiel Schweiz*, in: Samuel Mauch, Rolf Iten, Ernst U. von Weizsäcker and Jochen Jesinghaus, *Ökologische Steuerreform*, Rüegger Verlag: Zürich, 1992. See also Paul Johnson, Steve McKay and Stephen Smith, *The Distributional Consequences of Ecological Taxes*, Institute for Fiscal Studies: London, 1990.
25. Heike Förster, *Ökosteuern als Instrument der Umweltpolitik? Darstellung und Kritik einiger Vorschläge*, Deutscher Industrie-Verlag: Cologne, 1990.
26. Eckehard Bergmann and Dieter Ewringmann, *Ökosteuern: Entwicklung, Ansatzpunkte und Bewertung*, in Hans G. Nutzinger and Angelika Zahrnt (eds), *Umweltsteuern- und -abgaben in der Diskussion*, Müller: Karlsruhe, 1989, pp. 43-73.
27. Holger Bonus, *Marktwirtschaftliche Konzepte im Umwelt-schutz*, Ulmer: Stuttgart, 1984.
28. Commission of the European Communities, *A Community Strategy to Reduce Carbon Dioxide Emissions and to Improve Energy Efficiency*, SEC (91) 1744 final, 14 October, 1991.
29. Swedish Ministry of the Environment, *Economic Instruments in Sweden (with Emphasis on the Energy Sector)*, Regeringskansliets Offsetcentral; Stockholm, 1991
30. Business Council for Sustainable Development, *Changing Course*, Geneva, May 1992.

# Index